READY, SET, GO!

baby necessities to sew

Designs by Kristine Poor

Today's baby is a kiddo on the go, which often means Pumpkin's paraphernalia must be packed post-haste! Toward that end, these fun bags, bibs, blankets, and other necessities will provide peace of mind, as well as quick departures. There are four sets of projects to sew—a collection of shower gifts, and one set each for Mom, Dad, or Grandma. Each collection has at least one project to help with keeping it all together, such as a multi-pocket stroller caddy, oversized tote bag, or car seat organizer. These items are all machine-washable and no-fuss. That's because the World's Best Baby should be able to relax and enjoy every outing—and so should Mom, Dad, and Grandma.

LEISURE ARTS, INC.
Little Rock, Arkansas

EDITORIAL STAFF
EDITOR-IN-CHIEF: Susan White Sullivan
CRAFT PUBLICATIONS DIRECTOR:
    Cheryl Johnson
SPECIAL PROJECTS DIRECTOR:
    Susan Frantz Wiles
SENIOR PREPRESS DIRECTOR: Mark Hawkins
ART PUBLICATIONS DIRECTOR: Rhonda Shelby
TECHNICAL EDITOR: Lisa Lancaster
TECHNICAL WRITER: Frances Huddleston
EDITORIAL WRITER: Susan McManus Johnson
ART CATEGORY MANAGER: Lora Puls
LEAD GRAPHIC ARTIST: Angela Ormsby Stark
GRAPHIC ARTISTS: Jacob Casleton, Becca Snider,
    and Janie Marie Wright
IMAGING TECHNICIANS: Stephanie Johnson
    and Mark R. Potter
PHOTOGRAPHY DIRECTOR: Katherine Laughlin
CONTRIBUTING PHOTOGRAPHER: Ken West
CONTRIBUTING PHOTOSTYLIST: Sondra Daniel
PUBLISHING SYSTEMS ADMINISTRATOR:
    Becky Riddle
PUBLISHING SYSTEMS ASSISTANT:
    Clint Hanson
MAC INFORMATION TECHNOLOGY
    SPECIALIST: Robert Young

BUSINESS STAFF
VICE PRESIDENT AND CHIEF OPERATIONS
    OFFICER: Tom Siebenmorgen
DIRECTOR OF FINANCE AND
ADMINISTRATION: Laticia Mull Dittrich
VICE PRESIDENT, SALES AND MARKETING:
    Pam Stebbins
SALES DIRECTOR: Martha Adams
MARKETING DIRECTOR: Margaret Reinold
CREATIVE SERVICES DIRECTOR: Jeff Curtis
INFORMATION TECHNOLOGY DIRECTOR:
    Hermine Linz
CONTROLLER: Francis Caple
VICE PRESIDENT, OPERATIONS: Jim Dittrich
COMPTROLLER, OPERATIONS: Rob Thieme
RETAIL CUSTOMER SERVICE MANAGER:
    Stan Raynor
PRINT PRODUCTION MANAGER: Fred F. Pruss

Library of Congress Control Number: 2010925824

ISBN-13: 978-1-60140-993-5
ISBN-10: 1-60140-993-1

www.leisurearts.com

Kristine Poor

In 2006,
Kristine Poor
discovered
she had an
addiction—
she found she
couldn't stop
making bags! The
elation of seeing
each useful, colorful project completed
was simply irresistible. So she decided to
share the fun by selling the patterns she
developed. That's how Poorhouse Quilt
Designs got its start. Since then, Kristine
recruited her mother Jean Johnson as
pattern editor and creative assistant.
Kristine's design philosophy is based on
the view that quilters and sewers love to
expand their skills with smaller projects,
freeing them to experiment with color,
methods, and tools. In 2009, Kristine's
first Leisure Arts book, *Sew & Go Totes*
(#4751, LeisureArts.com), proved her
design theory by becoming an instant
success. To get handy sewing tips and
see what Kristine is currently working on,
visit her Web site and blog at
www.PoorhouseQuiltDesigns.com.

Table of Contents

Day Out with Dad

Today's dad is as adept at burping Baby and shopping for diapers as he is at assembling a new crib. For that do-it-all daddy, how about a stroller tote, changing pad, pacifier keeper, and bottle holder? Whether walking in the park or browsing the hardware store, Dad will be able to keep his tiny tyke in giggles and grins.

Stroll and Go Tote

Finished Tote Size: 14^1/$_2$" x 15^3/$_4$" x 2"
(37 cm x 40 cm x 5 cm)

> ***Tips:***
> *Spray your tote with a fabric protector (such as Scotchgard™) to repel spills and keep your tote looking new.*
> *Remove the straps and use the handles for a handy bag.*

YARDAGE REQUIREMENTS

Yardage is based on 43"/44" (109 cm/112 cm) wide fabric.

^{7}/$_8$ yd (80 cm) of green print fabric
^{7}/$_8$ yd (80 cm) of blue print fabric
^{1}/$_4$ yd (23 cm) of square print fabric

You will also need:

14" (36 cm) sport-weight zipper
2 yds (1.8 m) of 1" (25 mm) wide black webbing
^{3}/$_4$ yd (69 cm) of Pellon® Decor-Bond® fusible interfacing (45" [114 cm] wide)
Four 1^1/$_4$" (32 mm) D-rings
Four 1^1/$_4$" (32 mm) swivel clasps
Liquid fray preventative

CUTTING OUT THE PIECES

All measurements include $\frac{1}{4}$" seam allowances.

From green print fabric:
- Cut 1 **body** 17" x 34".
- Cut 1 **open pocket** $13\frac{1}{2}$" x $7\frac{1}{2}$".
- Cut 1 **zippered pocket** $13\frac{1}{2}$" x 6".
- Cut 1 **zippered pocket top** $13\frac{1}{2}$" x $2\frac{1}{2}$".

From blue print fabric:
- Cut 1 **body lining** 17" x 34".
- Cut 1 **open pocket lining** $13\frac{1}{2}$" x $7\frac{1}{2}$".
- Cut 1 **zippered pocket lining** $13\frac{1}{2}$" x 6".
- Cut 1 **zippered pocket top lining** $13\frac{1}{2}$" x $2\frac{1}{2}$".

From square print fabric:
- Cut 2 **trim strips** $2\frac{1}{2}$" x 40".

From Pellon® Decor-Bond®:
- Cut 1 **body interfacing** 17" x 34".
- Cut 1 **open pocket interfacing** $13\frac{1}{2}$" x $7\frac{1}{2}$".
- Cut 1 **zippered pocket interfacing** $13\frac{1}{2}$" x 6".

MAKING THE ZIPPERED POCKET

*Follow **Sewing** and **Pressing**, page 73, to make tote. Use a $\frac{1}{4}$" seam allowance throughout.*

1. Following manufacturer's instructions, fuse **zippered pocket interfacing** to **zippered pocket**.

2. Matching right sides, sew **zippered pocket** and **zippered pocket lining** together along both long edges. Turn pocket right side out. Roll pocket with fingers so that $\frac{3}{8}$" of lining shows across top of pocket; press.

Zippered Pocket

3. In the same manner, sew **zippered pocket top** and **zippered pocket top lining** together with $\frac{3}{8}$" of lining showing across bottom edge of pocket top.

Zippered Pocket Top

4. To shorten zipper, mark 13" from zipper pull on closed zipper (**Fig. 1**); stitch across zipper teeth several times at mark (shown in pink). Cut off end $\frac{1}{2}$" beyond stitching.

Fig. 1

5. Refer to **Fig. 2** to position zippered pocket close to zipper teeth; pin. Using zipper foot, center and topstitch 3 lines of stitching on exposed lining of zippered pocket.

Fig. 2

6. Refer to **Fig. 3** to position zippered pocket top close to zipper teeth; pin. Using zipper foot, center and topstitch 3 lines of stitching on exposed lining of zippered pocket top.

Fig. 3

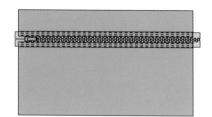

MAKING THE OPEN POCKET

1. Fuse **open pocket interfacing** to wrong side of **open pocket**.
2. Matching wrong sides, sew open pocket to **open pocket lining** along both long edges. Turn pocket right side out. In the same manner as zippered pocket, roll open pocket and topstitch exposed lining as shown.

Open Pocket

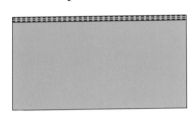

ADDING THE POCKETS

1. Fuse **body interfacing** to wrong side of **body**.
2. Refer to **Fig. 4** to center and pin pockets to 1 short end of body. Topstitch along side and bottom edges of open pocket. Stitch a divider line in center of pocket as shown or as desired. Topstitch along all outer edges of zippered pocket.

Fig. 4

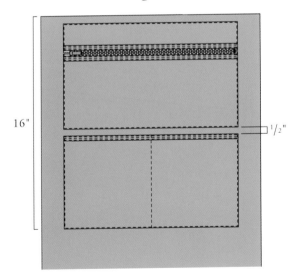

3. Matching wrong sides and long raw edges, press each **trim strip** in half. Align raw edges of 1 trim strip and pockets. Stitch trim strip to body ¼" from raw edges of trim strip (**Fig. 5**). Fold and press trim strip to outside; topstitch along each long edge of trim strip (**Fig. 6**). Trim ends of trim strip even with edges of body. Repeat to sew remaining trim strip to opposite side of pockets.

Fig. 5   **Fig. 6**

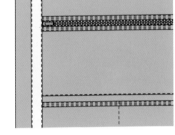

ADDING THE LOOPS AND HANDLES

1. Cut four 3" lengths of webbing for **loops** and two 12" lengths of webbing for **handles**. Apply fray preventative to cut ends.
2. Thread each loop through 1 D-ring and fold in half with cut ends matching.
3. Matching raw edges and referring to **Fig. 7**, baste 2 loops and 1 handle to 1 short edge of body. Repeat to baste 2 loops and 1 handle to remaining short edge of body.

Fig. 7

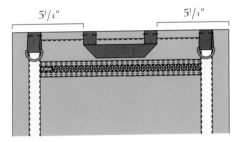

MAKING THE TOTE

1. With right sides together, sew **body** and **body lining** together along short edges; press seam allowances open.

2. Aligning seams between body and lining, fold body and lining as shown in **Fig. 8**. Sew side edges together, leaving an opening in lining for turning.

Fig. 8

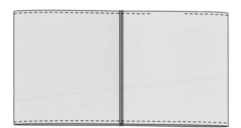

3. To box bottom of body, match right sides and align body side seams with center of body bottom. Refer to **Fig. 9** to sew across corner 1" from tip. Repeat for remaining side seam and bottom. Trim seam allowances to $1/4$".

Fig. 9

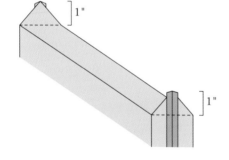

4. In the same manner, box bottom of body lining.

5. Turn body right side out and sew opening closed. Place lining inside body. Topstitch along top edge.

6. For **straps**, cut two 16" lengths of webbing. Apply fray preventative to cut ends. Thread each end through 1 swivel clasp and fold over 1". Using a short zigzag stitch, sew across each end to form loop.

Pacifier Keeper

Finished Keeper Size: 5¹/₂" x 4" (14 cm x 10 cm)

Tips:

Clip this keeper to a key ring to keep the pacifier handy!

To reduce bulk and save time, zigzag the seam allowances instead of binding them.

YARDAGE REQUIREMENTS

Yardage is based on 43"/44" (109 cm/112 cm) wide fabric.

Scrap or ¹/₄ yd (23 cm) of blue print fabric

Scrap or ¹/₄ yd (23 cm) of square print fabric

You will also need:

7" (18 cm) polyester all-purpose zipper

5" x 13" (13 cm x 33 cm) piece of medium-weight fusible interfacing

One 1" (25 mm) D-ring

CUTTING OUT THE PIECES

All measurements include ¹/₄" seam allowances.

From blue print fabric:

- Cut 2 **front/backs** 6" x 4¹/₂".

From square print fabric:

- Cut 2 **front/back linings** 6" x 4¹/₂".
- Cut 1 **seam binding strip** 1¹/₂" x 24".
- Cut 1 **rectangle** 2" x 3".

From medium-weight fusible interfacing:

- Cut 2 **front/back interfacings** 6" x 4¹/₂".

MAKING THE KEEPER

*Follow **Sewing** and **Pressing**, page 73, to make keeper. Use a ¹/₄" seam allowance throughout.*

1. Following manufacturer's instructions, fuse **front interfacing** to wrong side of **front**. Fuse **back interfacing** to wrong side of **back**.
2. Matching wrong sides, baste back and **back lining** together.
3. Use a pencil to draw a 5" x ³/₄" rectangle on interfacing side of front (**Fig. 1**).

Fig. 1

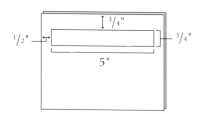

4. Matching right sides, layer **front lining** and front. Stitch along drawn lines. Making sure not to cut threads, make cuts inside stitching lines (**Fig. 2**).

Fig. 2

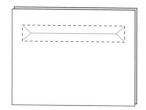

5. Turn right sides out, finger-pressing opening edges; press.
6. Position closed zipper behind opening. Using zipper foot and carefully stitching over teeth, topstitch zipper in place (**Fig. 3**). Trim zipper ends even with front.

Fig. 3

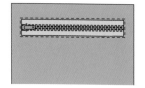

7. Matching wrong sides and short edges, fold **rectangle** in half and sew short edges together. Turn rectangle right side out to make **loop**. Topstitch along each long edge. Thread loop through D-ring and fold in half with short ends matching (**Fig. 4**).

Fig. 4

8. Matching raw edges, pin loop to right side of front 1" from left edge; baste loop in place (**Fig. 5**).

Fig. 5

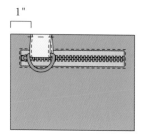

9. With zipper open and right sides matching, sew front and back together around all edges.
10. Matching wrong sides and long raw edges, press **seam binding strip** in half.
11. Follow **Attaching Binding with Mitered Corners**, page 79, to bind seam allowances. *Note: The instructions for **Attaching Binding with Mitered Corners** are for binding a quilt with figs. showing batting and backing extending beyond quilt top. Follow **Steps 1–7** and **9** as written, then topstitch binding along folded edge through all layers.*
12. Turn keeper right side out.

Bottle Holder

Finished Holder Size: 7¹/₂" high x 3" diameter (19 cm x 8 cm)

> **Tip:**
> Make an extra bottle holder for Dad's water bottle!

YARDAGE REQUIREMENTS

Yardage is based on 43"/44" (109 cm/112 cm) wide fabric.

- ³/₈ yd (34 cm) of green print fabric
- ³/₈ yd (34 cm) of green stripe fabric

You will also need:

- 12" (30 cm) sport-weight zipper
- 13" x 15" (33 cm x 38 cm) piece of insulated batting, such as Insul-Bright® by The Warm Company™
- Chalk pencil or water-soluble pen

CUTTING OUT THE PIECES

All measurements include ¹/₄" seam allowances.
Top/bottom patterns are on page 70.

From green print fabric:
- Cut 1 **body** 11¹/₂" x 10".
- Cut 2 **top/bottoms** from pattern.
- Cut 1 **handle** 1¹/₂" x 4¹/₂".
- Cut 1 **seam binding strip** 2" x 10".
- Cut 2 **zipper end covers** 1¹/₂" x 3¹/₂".

From green stripe fabric:
- Cut 1 **body lining** 11¹/₂" x 10".
- Cut 2 **top/bottom linings** from pattern.
- Cut 1 **handle lining** 1¹/₂" x 4¹/₂".
- Cut 2 **accent strips** 2" x 12".

From insulated batting:
- Cut 1 **body batting** 11¹/₂" x 10".
- Cut 2 **top/bottom battings** from pattern.

MAKING THE ZIPPER ASSEMBLY

*Follow **Sewing** and **Pressing**, page 73, to make holder. Use a ¹/₄" seam allowance throughout.*

1. Matching wrong sides and short raw edges, fold 1 **zipper end cover** in half and sew short edges together. Turn cover right side out to form a loop. Fold 1 raw edge ¹/₂" to the inside of loop; press (**Fig. 1**). Repeat with remaining zipper end cover.

Fig. 1

2. Insert each end of zipper into folded end of 1 zipper end cover. Place 1 cover ¹/₂" above zipper stop. Adjust placement of remaining cover until covers are 9" apart. Stitch along folded edge of each cover (**Fig. 2**). Trim end of zipper even with outer edge of cover.

Fig. 2

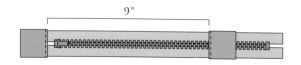

MAKING THE BOTTLE HOLDER BODY

1. Layer **body lining**, right side down, **body batting**, shiny side down, and **body**, right side up; baste layers together. Follow **Quilting**, page 75, to quilt body with quilting lines stitched parallel to short edges of body and spaced 1" apart.

2. Trim body to 10" x 8".

3. Cut across body 2" from 1 long edge (**Fig. 3**) to make **upper body** (10" x 2") and **lower body** (10" x 6").

Fig. 3

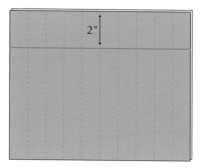

4. Matching wrong sides and long raw edges, press each **accent strip** in half.

5. Use accent strips and follow **Attaching Open End Binding**, page 78, to bind 1 long (bottom) edge of upper body and 1 long (top) edge of lower body (**Fig. 4**).

Fig. 4

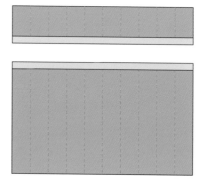

6. Refer to **Fig. 5** to position upper body, right side up, close to zipper teeth on closed zipper, pin. Using zipper foot, topstitch along each edge of accent strip.

Fig. 5

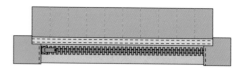

7. Refer to **Fig. 6** to position lower body, right side up, on remaining zipper tape close to zipper teeth. Topstitch along each edge of accent strip (**Fig. 6**). Trim zipper and zipper end covers even with edges of upper and lower body.

Fig. 6

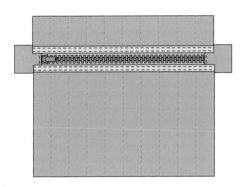

8. Matching right sides and short raw edges, sew short edges of body together.
9. Matching wrong sides and long raw edges, press **seam binding strip** in half.
10. Follow **Attaching Open End Binding**, page 78, to bind seam allowances.

MAKING THE BOTTLE HOLDER TOP AND BOTTOM

1. Layer **top lining**, right side down, **top batting**, shiny side down and centered, and **top**, right side up. With walking foot, baste layers together $1/8$" from outer edges. Repeat with **bottom lining**, **bottom batting**, and **bottom**.

COMPLETING THE BOTTLE HOLDER

1. Matching right sides, sew **handle** and **handle lining** together along long edges. Turn handle right side out. Topstitch along each long edge.

2. Refer to **Fig. 7** and use chalk pencil or water-soluble pen to mark dots at 4 equal points $1/4$" from edges of lining side of top. Repeat to make 4 dots on lining side of bottom.

Fig. 7

3. Matching raw edges, with right sides facing up, and with handle ends centered over 2 opposite dots on top, baste ends of handle to top (**Fig. 8**).

Fig. 8

4. Beginning at seam, mark dots at 4 equal points on lining side of body $1/4$" from each end.
5. Matching dots and right sides and with ends of handle centered over dots on either side of seam, pin top to body. Sew top and body together. Zigzag seam allowances.
6. Un-zip zipper. In the same manner as top, sew bottom to body. Turn bottle holder right side out.

Changing Pad

Finished Pad Size: 15¼" x 19¼"
(39 cm x 49 cm)

YARDAGE REQUIREMENTS

Yardage is based on 43"/44"
(109 cm/112 cm) wide fabric.
- ½ yd (46 cm) of square print fabric
- ½ yd (46 cm) of green print fabric

You will also need:
- 16" x 20" (41 cm x 51 cm) piece of fusible fleece
- 16" x 20" (41 cm x 51 cm) piece of iron-on vinyl

CUTTING OUT THE PIECES

Measurements include ⅜" seam allowances.

From square print fabric:
- Cut 1 **pad** 16" x 20".

From green print fabric:
- Cut 1 **pad lining** 16" x 20".

MAKING THE PAD

*Follow **Sewing** and **Pressing**, page 73, to make pad.*

1. Following manufacturer's instructions, fuse fleece to *wrong* side of **pad**. Follow **Quilting**, page 75, to quilt pad if desired. Pad shown was meander quilted.

2. Following manufacturer's instructions, fuse iron-on vinyl to *right* side of **pad lining**.

3. Layer **pad**, fleece side down, and **pad lining**, vinyl side down. Using a ⅜" seam allowance and leaving an opening for turning, sew pad and pad lining together.

4. Clip corners and turn pad right side out. Sew opening closed.

5. Zigzag around pad close to edges.

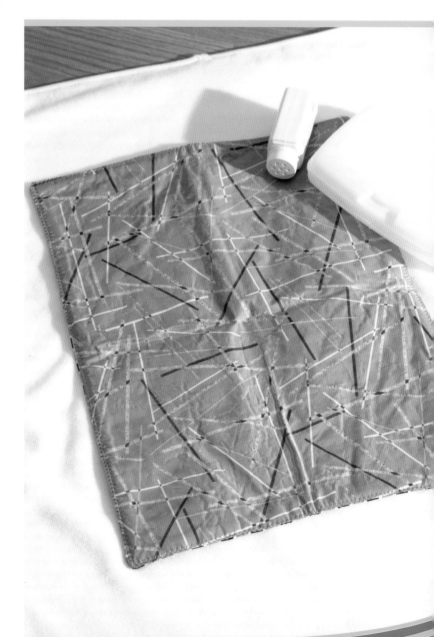

On the Go Mom

You know how it is—the work at home. The work at work. The work of getting to work and back home. Then this little person comes along, melting your heart while messing up your schedule. Good thing you have your messenger bag, toy tote, diaper clutch/changing pad, and handy car seat organizer. They can help smooth out some of the bumps in your day, while that amazing new kid makes it all worthwhile.

Mom's Messenger Bag

Finished Bag Size: 14^1/$_2$" x 13" x 5"
(37 cm x 33 cm x 13 cm)

Tip:
Substitute two packages of purchased piping instead of making your own.

YARDAGE REQUIREMENTS
Yardage is based on 43"/44"
(109 cm/112 cm) wide fabric.

   1 yd (91 cm) of navy floral print fabric

   1^1/$_8$ yds (1 m) of navy small print fabric

   ^{7}/$_8$ yd (80 cm) of square print fabric

   ^{5}/$_8$ yd (57 cm) of blue dot fabric

You will also need:

   ^{3}/$_4$ yds (69 cm) of fusible fleece (45" [114 cm] wide)

   ^{5}/$_8$ yd (57 cm) of insulated batting, such as Insul-Bright® by The Warm Company™ (22" [56 cm] wide)

   2^1/$_4$ yds (2.1 m) of medium-weight fusible interfacing (20" [51 cm] wide)

   ^{7}/$_8$ yd (80 cm) of ^{3}/$_8$" (10 mm) wide elastic

   3 yds (2.7 m) of ^{4}/$_{32}$" (3 mm) diameter piping cord

   Two 1^1/$_2$" (38 mm) D-rings

CUTTING OUT THE PIECES
All measurements include ^{1}/$_4$" *seam allowances.*

From navy floral print fabric:
- Cut 1 **front/back** 15" x 31".
- Cut 2 **outside bottle pockets** 5^1/$_2$" x 7".
- Cut 1 **large rectangle** 9^1/$_2$" x 10^1/$_2$".
- Cut 2 **side panels** 5^1/$_2$" x 13^1/$_2$".

From navy small print fabric:
- Cut 1 **front/back lining** 15" x 31".
- Cut 1 **flap lining** 15" x 10^1/$_2$".
- Cut 2 **outside bottle pocket linings** 5^1/$_2$" x 7".
- Cut 1 **short strap** 4" x 10".
- Cut 1 **long strap** 4" x 40".

From square print fabric:
- Cut 2 **organizer pockets** 15" x 7".
- Cut 2 **organizer pocket linings** 15" x 7".
- Cut 2 **inside bottle pockets** 8" x 9".
- Cut 2 **inside bottle pocket linings** 8" x 9".
- Cut 1 **small rectangle** 6" x 10$\frac{1}{2}$".
- Cut 2 **side panel linings** 5$\frac{1}{2}$" x 13$\frac{1}{2}$".

From blue dot fabric:
- Cut 1 **facing** 2$\frac{1}{2}$" x 44", pieced as needed.
- Cut 1 **square for piping** 15" x 15".
- Cut 2 **casings** 1$\frac{1}{2}$" x 8".

From fusible fleece:
- Cut 1 **front/back fleece** 15" x 31".
- Cut 1 **flap fleece** 15" x 10$\frac{1}{2}$".
- Cut 1 **long strap fleece** 3" x 38".
- Cut 1 **short strap fleece** 3" x 8".

From insulated batting:
- Cut 2 **inside bottle pocket battings** 8" x 9".
- Cut 2 **side panel battings** 5$\frac{1}{2}$" x 13$\frac{1}{2}$".

From medium-weight fusible interfacing:
- Cut 1 **front/back interfacing** 15" x 31".
- Cut 2 **organizer pocket interfacings** 15" x 7".
- Cut 1 **flap interfacing** 15" x 10$\frac{1}{2}$".
- Cut 2 **outside bottle pocket interfacings** 5$\frac{1}{2}$" x 7".
- Cut 2 **side panel interfacings** 5$\frac{1}{2}$" x 13$\frac{1}{2}$".

MAKING THE STRAPS

*Follow **Sewing** and **Pressing**, page 73. Use a $\frac{1}{4}$" seam allowance throughout.*

1. Following manufacturer's instructions, center and fuse **long strap fleece** to wrong side of **long strap**.
2. Press 1 short edge and then both long edges of long strap $\frac{1}{2}$" to wrong side (**Fig. 1**).

Fig. 1

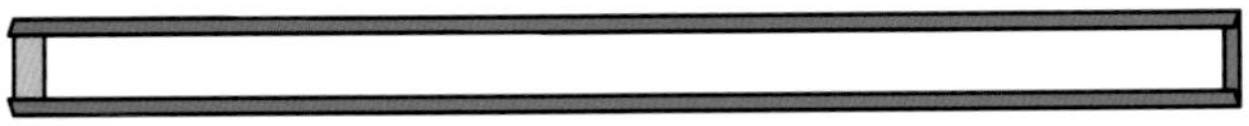

3. Press long strap in half lengthwise. Topstitch along folded edges and $\frac{1}{4}$" from folded edges (**Fig. 2**).

Fig. 2

4. Repeat **Steps 1–3** using **short strap** and **short strap fleece**.
5. Thread finished end of long strap through D-rings. Fold finished end of strap 2$\frac{1}{4}$" to wrong side and topstitch in place (**Fig. 3**).

Fig. 3

MAKING THE PIPING

1. Use **square for piping** and follow **Making a Continuous Bias Strip**, page 76, to make approximately 3 yds of 1$\frac{1}{4}$"w **bias strip**.
2. Lay piping cord along center of bias strip on wrong side of fabric; fold strip over cord. Using zipper foot, stitch close to cord. Trim seam allowances to $\frac{1}{4}$".

MAKING THE FLAP

1. Matching right sides and one long edge, sew **small rectangle** and **large rectangle** together (**Fig. 4**) to make **flap**.

Fig. 4

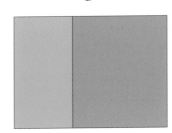

2. Fuse **flap fleece** to wrong side of flap. Follow **Quilting**, page 75, to quilt as desired. Bag shown was meander quilted.

3. To round corners of **flap**, place a drinking glass or lid, approximately 4" in diameter, on one corner of flap and draw around glass or lid (**Fig. 5**); trim along drawn line. Repeat for remaining corner on same long edge.

Fig. 5

4. Using zipper foot and matching raw edges, baste piping to right side of flap along side and bottom (curved) edges (**Fig. 6**). To make basting around curves easier, clip seam allowances of piping at rounded flap corners.

Fig. 6

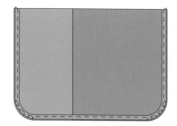

5. Following manufacturer's instructions, fuse **flap interfacing** to wrong side of **flap lining**. Using the 4" diameter drinking glass or lid, round bottom corners in the same manner as corners of flap.

6. Using zipper foot, matching right sides, and stitching as close as possible to cord, sew flap and flap lining together along side and bottom edges.

7. Turn flap right side out; press. Baste top raw edges together (**Fig. 7**).

Fig. 7

MAKING THE FRONT/BACK

1. Fuse **front/back fleece** to wrong side of **front/back** and quilt as desired. Bag shown was meander quilted.

MAKING THE SIDE PANELS

1. Fuse 1 **outside bottle pocket interfacing** to wrong side of each **outside bottle pocket**.

2. Matching right sides and raw edges, sew 1 **outside bottle pocket** and 1 **outside bottle pocket lining** together along 1 short (top) edge. Turn pocket right side out; press. Topstitch along fold and $1/4$" from fold. Repeat with remaining outside bottle pocket and outside bottle pocket lining.

3. Fuse 1 **side panel interfacing** to wrong side of each **side panel**.

4. Matching side and bottom edges and with right sides facing up, baste 1 **outside bottle pocket** to each **side panel** (**Fig. 8**). Using a drinking glass or lid with a diameter of approximately $2^{1}/8$", round bottom corners of each **side panel** in the same manner as corners on flap (**Fig. 9**).

Fig. 8	Fig. 9

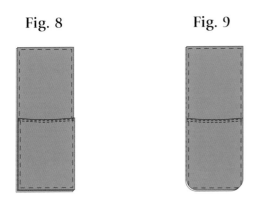

MAKING THE INSIDE BOTTLE POCKETS

1. Layer 1 **inside bottle pocket lining**, right side down, 1 **inside bottle pocket batting**, shiny side down, and 1 **inside bottle pocket**, right side up. Baste layers together. Repeat with remaining inside bottle pocket, batting, and lining.

2. Using the $2^1/8$" diameter drinking glass or lid, round bottom corners of inside bottle pockets (**Fig. 12**).

5. Using zipper foot and matching raw edges, baste piping to right side of each side panel along side and bottom (curved) edges. Clip seam allowances of piping at rounded panel corners as needed (**Fig. 10**).

Fig. 12

Fig. 10

3. For elastic casings, press 1 long edge of each **casing** $1/4$" to wrong side.

4. Matching raw edges and right side of casing to lining side of pocket, sew 1 casing to top edge of 1 inside bottle pocket (**Fig. 13**). Fold casing to right side. Topstitch along folded edge of casing (**Fig. 14**). Repeat to sew casing to remaining inside bottle pocket.

6. Cut a $3^1/2$" length of elastic. Stretching elastic across top edge on wrong side of 1 side panel, zigzag stretched elastic to side panel (**Fig. 11**). Repeat with remaining side panel.

Fig. 13	Fig. 14

Fig. 11

5. Cut a 6" length of elastic. Attach a safety pin at 1 end of elastic; insert into casing. Stitch over ends of casing to hold elastic in place (**Fig. 15**). Repeat with remaining casing.

Fig. 15

6. Baste $1/8$" and $1/4$" from edge along bottom of each inside bottle pocket (between curves) for gathering.

MAKING THE SIDE PANEL LININGS

1. Layer 1 **side panel batting**, shiny side up, and 1 **side panel lining**, right side up; baste layers together. Repeat with remaining side panel batting and side panel lining.
2. Using the $2^1/8$" diameter drinking glass or lid, round bottom corners of each side panel lining (**Fig. 16**).

Fig. 16

3. Gathering basting threads on inside bottle pocket to fit side panel lining and with right sides facing up, baste 1 **inside bottle pocket** and 1 **side panel lining** together along side and bottom (curved) edges (**Fig. 17**).

Fig. 17

4. Cut a $3^1/2$" length of elastic. Stretching elastic across top edge on batting side of 1 side panel lining, zigzag stretched elastic to side panel lining (**Fig. 18**). Repeat with remaining side panel lining.

Fig. 18

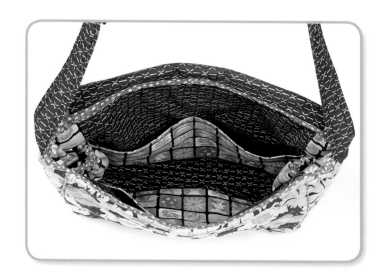

MAKING THE ORGANIZER POCKETS

1. Fuse 1 **organizer pocket interfacing** to wrong side of each **organizer pocket**.
2. Matching right sides and raw edges, sew 1 **organizer pocket** and 1 **organizer pocket lining** together along both long edges. Repeat with remaining organizer pocket and lining.
3. Turn each organizer pocket right side out; press. Topstitch along one long (top) edge and ¼" from top edge (**Fig. 19**).

Fig. 19

MAKING THE FRONT/BACK LINING

1. Fuse **front/back interfacing** to wrong side of **front/back lining**.
2. Pin 1 organizer pocket 6" from each short edge of front/back lining (**Fig. 20**). Topstitch pockets to lining along bottom edges of pockets. Baste sides of pockets to lining. Stitch divider lines in pockets as shown or as desired.

Fig. 20

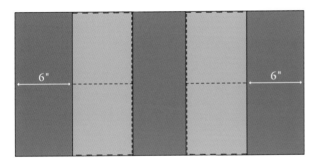

ASSEMBLING THE MESSENGER BAG

1. Matching right sides, sew **side panel linings** to **front/back lining** (Fig. 21).

Fig. 21

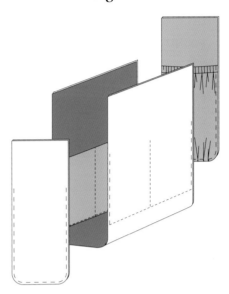

2. Matching right sides, using zipper foot, and sewing as close as possible to cord, sew **side panels** to **front/back** (**Fig. 22**). Turn bag right side out.

Fig. 22

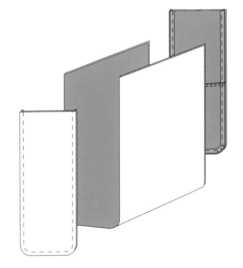

3. Matching wrong sides, place lining inside outer bag and baste layers together along top edge.

4. Matching right sides and raw edges, baste **flap** to top edge of bag back (**Fig. 23**).

Fig. 23

5. Matching raw edges and stretching elastic at top of bag sides as you stitch, baste **long strap** and **short strap** to top edge of bag sides (**Fig. 24**).

Fig. 24

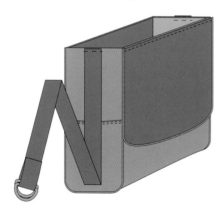

6. Matching wrong sides and long raw edges, press **facing** in half. Press one end of facing diagonally (**Fig. 25**).

Fig. 25

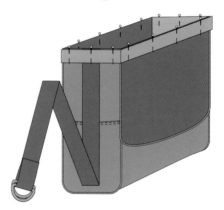

7. Beginning with pressed end of facing and matching raw edges, pin facing around top edges of bag and flap (**Fig. 26**). Overlap ends by 2"; trim excess facing. Sew facing to bag.

Fig. 26

8. Turn bag wrong side out and fold facing over seam allowances to lining. Stitching through all layers, topstitch along bottom edge of facing.

9. Turn bag right side out. Weave loose end of short strap through D-rings.

Car Organizer

Finished Organizer Size: 15^1/$_2$" x 23^1/$_2$"
(39 cm x 60 cm)

> *Tip*
> *Pockets can be made from medium weight polyester mesh. Using mesh will allow the user to see what items are in the organizer.*

YARDAGE REQUIREMENTS

Yardage is based on 43"/44"
(109 cm/112 cm) wide fabric.

^{3}/$_4$ yd (69 cm) of navy solid fabric
^{3}/$_8$ yd (34 cm) of green print fabric
^{1}/$_2$ yd (46 cm) of blue stripe fabric
^{5}/$_8$ yd (57 cm) of navy floral fabric
^{1}/$_4$ yd (23 cm) of blue dot fabric

You will also need:

^{3}/$_4$ yd (69 cm) Pellon® Peltex®70 heavy-weight fusible interfacing (20" [51 cm] wide)
Four 1" (25 mm) D-rings
^{3}/$_4$ yd (69 cm) of ^{1}/$_2$" (13 mm) wide elastic
2^3/$_4$ yds (2.5 m) of 1" (25 mm) wide navy webbing
Chalk pencil or water-soluble marker
Liquid fray preventative

CUTTING OUT THE PIECES

All measurements include seam allowances.

From navy solid fabric:
- Cut 1 **front** 16^1/$_2$" x 24^1/$_2$".
- Cut 1 **back** 16^1/$_2$" x 24^1/$_2$".

From green print fabric:
- Cut 1 **top pocket** 22^1/$_2$" x 10^1/$_2$".

From blue stripe print fabric:
- Cut 1 **middle pocket** 40" x 15".

From navy floral fabric:
- Cut 1 **bottom pocket** 40" x 17".

From blue dot fabric:
- Cut 1 **binding strip** 2^1/$_2$" x 24^1/$_2$".
- Cut 2 **casings** 1^3/$_4$" x 40".

From Pellon® Peltex®70:
- Cut 1 **front interfacing** 15^1/$_2$" x 23^1/$_2$".

MAKING THE FRONT

*Follow **Sewing** and **Pressing**, page 73. Use a ¹/₄" seam allowance unless otherwise indicated.*

1. Following manufacturer's instructions, center and fuse **front interfacing** to wrong side of **front**.

MAKING THE TOP POCKET

1. Matching wrong sides and long raw edges, fold **top pocket** in half; press.
2. Matching wrong sides and long raw edges, press **binding strip** in half.
3. Follow **Attaching Open End Binding**, page 78, to bind long raw edge (top) of top pocket.
4. Using chalk pencil or water-soluble pen, mark lines on top pocket as shown in **Fig. 1**. Topstitch along each line from bottom edge of pocket to bottom edge of binding.

Fig. 1

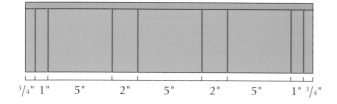

³/₄" 1"   5"   2"   5"   2"   5"   1" ³/₄"

5. Folding pocket at topstitched lines, press pleats as shown in **Fig. 2**.

Fig. 2

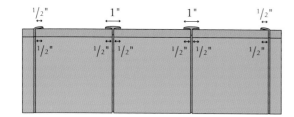

MAKING THE MIDDLE AND BOTTOM POCKETS

1. Matching wrong sides and long raw edges, fold **middle pocket** in half; press.
2. Press one long edge of 1 **casing** ¹/₂" to wrong side.
3. Matching long raw edges and right side of casing to wrong side of pocket, sew casing to middle pocket (**Fig. 3**). Fold casing to right side of pocket encasing seam allowances. Topstitch along bottom edge of pocket casing (**Fig. 4**).

Fig. 3   **Fig. 4**

4. Cut a 12" length of elastic. Attach a safety pin at 1 end of elastic length; insert into casing. Stitch over ends of casing to hold elastic in place (**Fig. 5**).

Fig. 5

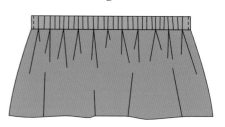

5. Baste ¹/₈" and ¹/₄" from fold at bottom of middle pocket for gathering.
6. Repeat **Steps 1–5** to make **bottom pocket**.

MAKING THE STRAPS

1. From webbing, cut 2 **lower straps** 6" long and 2 **upper straps** 42" long. Apply fray preventative to cut ends.
2. Thread 1 lower strap through 2 D-rings and match ends. Baste ends together ¼" from cut edges (**Fig. 6**). Repeat with remaining lower strap.

Fig. 6

ASSEMBLING THE ORGANIZER

1. Using chalk pencil or water-soluble pen, mark lines on **front** as shown (**Fig. 7**).

Fig. 7

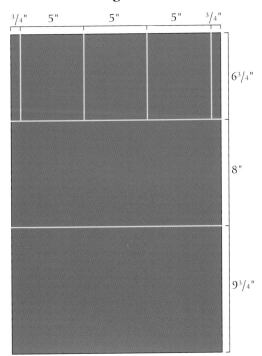

2. Matching side edges and with right sides facing up, align bottom edge of **top pocket** with upper horizontal line on front. Baste top pocket to front along side edges. Align pleats on pocket with vertical lines on front (**Fig. 8**). Stitch divider lines in pocket using lines on front as guides.

Fig. 8

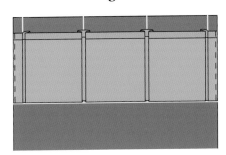

3. Pin pressed pleats in place along bottom edge of pocket and topstitch along bottom edge of pocket.
4. Gather basting threads on **middle pocket** to 16½". Matching right sides and side edges, align bottom edge of middle pocket with lower horizontal line on front. Sew middle pocket to front along gathered edge (**Fig. 9**).

Fig. 9

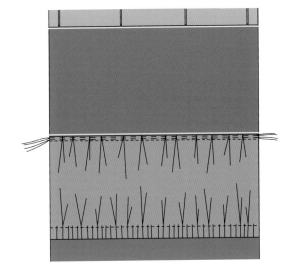

5. Fold pocket up and stretching elastic as needed, baste middle pocket to front along side edges. Stitch a divider line in center of pocket as shown (**Fig. 10**) or as desired.

Fig. 10

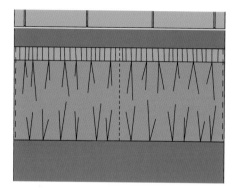

6. Gather basting threads on **bottom pocket** to 16$^1/_2$". Aligning side and bottom edges and with right sides facing up, baste bottom pocket to front along side and bottom edges (**Fig. 11**).

Fig. 11

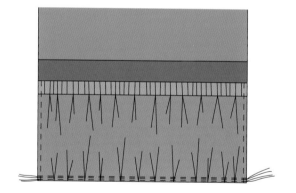

7. Referring to **Fig. 12** for placement, match right sides and raw edges and sew 2 **upper straps** and 2 **lower straps** to front.

Fig. 12

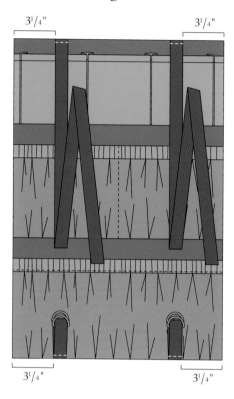

8. Using a $^1/_2$" seam allowance, matching right sides and raw edges, and pinning straps out of the way as needed, sew **front** and **back** together along side and bottom edges. Turn organizer right side out and sew top opening closed.

Quick Change Diaper Clutch

Finished Clutch Size: 17" x 24" (43 cm x 61 cm) open; 7" x 9" (18 cm x 23 cm) folded

Tips
Before you get started, read the manufacturer's instructions for the iron-on vinyl product.
Using your walking foot will make sewing the vinyl easier.

YARDAGE REQUIREMENTS

Yardage is based on 43"/44" (109 cm/112 cm) wide fabric.

$5/8$ yd (57 cm) of square print fabric
$5/8$ yd (57 cm) of blue dot fabric
$3/8$ yd (34 cm) of navy print fabric

You will also need:

$5/8$ yd (57 cm) of fusible fleece (45" [114 cm] wide)
$1/4$ yd (23 cm) of medium-weight fusible interfacing (44" [112 cm] wide)
$3/4$ yd (69 cm) of iron-on vinyl (17" [43 cm] wide)
Chalk pencil or water-soluble marker

CUTTING OUT THE PIECES

All measurements include $1/4$" seam allowances.

From square print fabric:
- Cut 1 **outer clutch** 17" x 24".

From blue dot fabric:
- Cut 1 **clutch lining** 17" x 24".
- Cut 1 **pocket** 17" x $6^1/2$".
- Cut 1 **pocket lining** 17" x $6^1/2$".

From navy print fabric:
- Cut 4 **strips** $2^1/2$"w.

From fusible fleece:
- Cut 1 **clutch fleece** 17" x 24".

From medium-weight fusible interfacing:
- Cut 1 **pocket interfacing** 17" x $6^1/2$".

From iron-on vinyl:
- Cut 1 **clutch vinyl** 17" x 24".

MAKING THE DIAPER CLUTCH

*Follow **Sewing** and **Pressing**, page 73. Use a $1/4$" seam allowance throughout. Follow manufacturer's instructions to fuse vinyl, fleece, and interfacing to fabric pieces.*

1. Fuse **clutch vinyl** to *right* side of **clutch lining**.
2. Fuse **clutch fleece** to *wrong* side of **outer clutch**.

3. On right side of outer clutch, use chalk pencil or water-soluble pen to mark lines as shown in **Fig. 1**.

Fig. 1

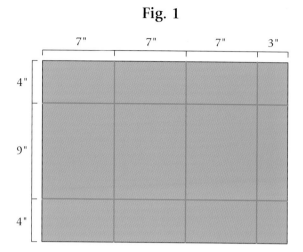

4. Layer **outer clutch**, right side down, and **clutch lining**, right side up. Baste layers together along outer edges. Topstitch along all marked lines.
5. Fuse **pocket interfacing** to *wrong* side of **pocket**.
6. Matching right sides, sew pocket and **pocket lining** together along 1 long edge. Turn pocket right side out, and topstitch along sewn edge.
7. Matching raw edges and with pocket facing up, baste sides and bottom of **pocket** to vinyl side of clutch (**Fig. 2**).

Fig. 2

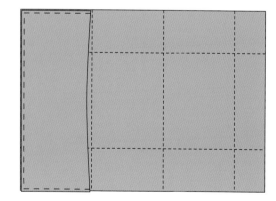

8. Trim corners of clutch as shown in **Fig. 3**.

Fig. 3

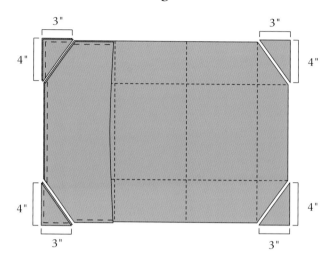

9. Using diagonal seams (**Fig. 4**), sew 3 **strips** together end to end for **binding**. Matching wrong sides and long edges, press binding in half.

Fig. 4

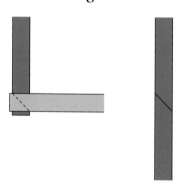

10. Follow **Attaching Continuous Binding**, page 77, to bind clutch.

11. From remaining **strip**, cut a 30" length for **tie**. Matching wrong sides and long edges, press tie in half; unfold. Press short ends ¹/₂" to wrong side. Press long raw edges to wrong side to meet pressed crease (**Fig. 5**). Press tie in half again. Topstitch along all edges (**Fig. 6**).

Fig. 5

Fig. 6

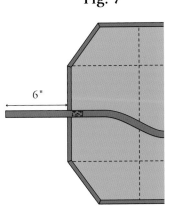

12. Referring to **Fig. 7**, sew **tie** to outer clutch at bottom of pocket.

Fig. 7

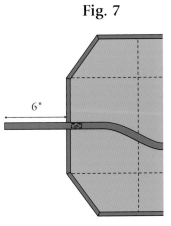

6"

Fig. 9

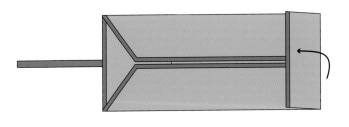

Fig. 10

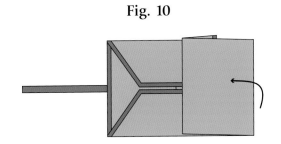

13. To close clutch, follow **Figs. 8–11** to fold along topstitched lines. Tie closed.

Fig. 8

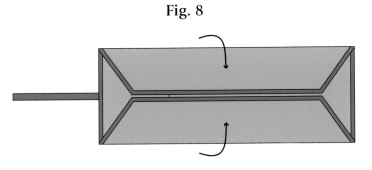

Fig. 11

Toy Tote

Finished Tote Size: 11¹/₂" x 12" x 3" (29 cm x 30 cm x 8 cm)

Tip:
Substitute rickrack for the flanges on the front and back of tote.

YARDAGE REQUIREMENTS

Yardage is based on 43"/44" (109 cm/112 cm) wide fabric.

⁵/₈ yd (57 cm) of navy floral print fabric

⁷/₈ yd (80 cm) of navy small print fabric

³/₈ yd (34 cm) of green print fabric

¹/₈ yd (11 cm) of blue stripe fabric

¹/₈ yd (11 cm) of blue dot fabric

You will also need:

¹/₂ yd (46 cm) of fusible fleece (45" [114 cm] wide)

1 yd (91 cm) of 1" (25 mm) wide navy webbing

Liquid fray preventative

CUTTING OUT THE PIECES

All measurements include seam allowances.

From navy floral print fabric:
- Cut 4 **tote sides** 5" x 11¹/₂".
- Cut 2 **pocket linings** 15¹/₂" x 6".

From navy small print fabric:
- Cut 1 **tote lining** 15¹/₂" x 27¹/₂".
- Cut 1 **tote bottom** 15¹/₂" x 5¹/₂".
- Cut 4 **flanges** 1" x 11¹/₂".
- Cut 2 **pocket trims** 1" x 15¹/₂".

From green print fabric:
- Cut 2 **large rectangles** 4¹/₂" x 8".
- Cut 2 **pockets** 15¹/₂" x 6".

From blue stripe fabric:
- Cut 2 **small rectangles** 4¹/₂" x 4".

From blue dot fabric:
- Cut 2 **long rectangles** 2¹/₂" x 11¹/₂".

From fusible fleece:
- Cut 1 **tote fleece** 15¹/₂" x 27¹/₂".
- Cut 2 **pocket fleeces** 15¹/₂" x 5".

MAKING THE TOTE FRONT AND BACK

*Follow **Sewing** and **Pressing**, page 73. Use a ¼" seam allowance unless otherwise indicated.*

1. Sew 1 **small rectangle** and 1 **large rectangle** together to make **Unit 1**. Make 2 Unit 1's.

Unit 1 (make 2)

2. Sew 1 **Unit 1** and 1 **long rectangle** together to make **Unit 2**. Make 2 Unit 2's.

Unit 2 (make 2)

3. Matching wrong sides and long raw edges, press each **flange** in half.

4. Matching right sides and raw edges, sew 1 flange to each side (left and right) of Unit 2 (**Fig. 1**). Repeat to sew flanges to sides of remaining Unit 2.

Fig. 1

5. Sew 2 **tote sides** and 1 Unit 2 together with flange sandwiched in between to make **tote front**. Press flanges to Unit 2. Baste flanges in place along top and bottom edges of tote front. Repeat to make **tote back**.

Tote Front/Back (make 2)

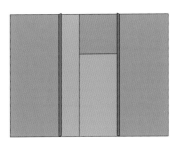

MAKING THE TOTE BODY

1. Place **tote fleece**, fusible side up, on work surface. Aligning top edge of **tote front** with 1 short edge of fleece, place front, right side up, on top of fleece (**Fig. 2**); pin in place.

Fig. 2

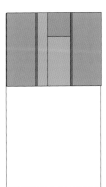

2. Matching right sides and bottom raw edge of tote front with 1 long edge of **tote bottom** and stitching through all layers, sew tote bottom to tote front (**Fig. 3**). Fold tote bottom open and finger press seam (**Fig. 4**).

Fig. 3 **Fig. 4**

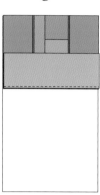 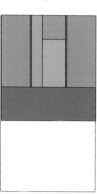

3. Matching right sides and bottom raw edge of **tote back** with remaining long edge of **tote bottom** and stitching through all layers, sew tote back to tote bottom (**Fig. 5**). Fold tote back open and finger press seam (**Fig. 6**).

Fig. 5 **Fig. 6**

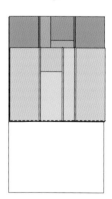 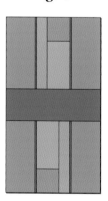

4. Folding tote front and back out of the way, trim $1/2$" from both short edges of tote fleece.
5. Following manufacturer's instructions, fuse tote fleece to tote front/back and bottom to make **tote body**.
6. Cut two 15" lengths of webbing for **handles**. Apply fray preventative to cut ends.
7. Matching right sides, centering handle ends over flanges, and extending handle ends $3/4$" beyond edge of tote front, sew 1 handle to tote front $1/4$" from edge of tote front (**Fig. 7**). Repeat to sew remaining handle to tote back.

Fig. 7

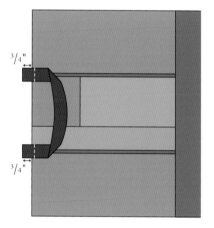

8. Using $1/2$" seam allowances and matching right sides and short (top) edges of tote body, sew side seams.

MAKING THE TOTE LINING
1. Center and fuse 1 **pocket fleece** to wrong side of each **pocket lining**.
2. Matching wrong sides and long raw edges, press each **pocket trim** in half.
3. Matching right sides and raw edges, sew 1 pocket trim to 1 long edge (top) of each pocket lining.

4. Matching right sides and long raw edges and with trim sandwiched in between, sew 1 pocket lining to each **pocket** along top edge. Turn pockets right side out (**Fig. 8**). Baste bottom raw edges together.

Fig. 8

5. Matching side edges and with lining and pockets facing up, pin 1 pocket 6^1/$_2$" from each short edge of **tote lining**. Topstitch pockets to lining along bottom edges. Baste sides of pockets to lining. Topstitch divider lines in pockets as shown or as desired (**Fig. 9**).

Fig. 9

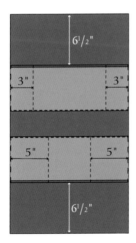

6. Using ^{1}/$_2$" seam allowances, matching right sides and short edges of tote lining, and leaving a 4" opening in center of one side for turning, sew sides of tote lining together.

COMPLETING THE TOTE

1. To box bottom of tote body, match right sides and align tote side seams with center of tote bottom. Refer to **Fig. 10** to sew across corner 1^1/$_2$" from tip. Trim seam allowances to ^{1}/$_4$". Repeat for remaining side seam and bottom. Turn tote body right side out.

Fig. 10

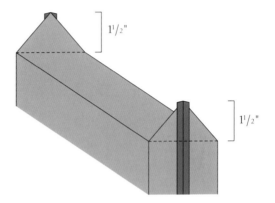

2. In the same manner, box bottom of tote lining. Do not turn tote lining right side out.
3. Matching right sides and top edges, place tote body inside tote lining. Sew tote body and tote lining together along top edges. Turn tote right side out through opening in lining. Sew opening closed. Place lining inside tote.
4. Topstitch around tote along top edge and ^{1}/$_2$" from top edge.

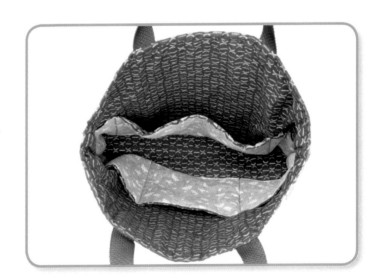

Play Date at Grandma's

Alright! Baby gets to spend time today with the best gal in the world—Grandma! She's got everything ready for a fun-filled visit. There's a cushy ball with ribbon loops for little fingers to grab. And look—a set of soft blocks to stack or toss. She's even got a small security blanket to soothe any naptime anxieties. For all other concerns, there's a nifty diaper daypack with pockets for necessities. When it comes to organization, Grandma's got game!

Diaper Daypack

Finished Daypack Size:
13$\frac{1}{2}$" x 13$\frac{1}{2}$" x 5"
(34 cm x 34 cm x 13 cm)

Tips:

When choosing fabrics, choose a lighter color fabric for the lining so it will be easier to see items in your bag.

Before fusing interfacing or fleece to fabric, place parchment paper on your ironing board to protect the board covering.

YARDAGE REQUIREMENTS

Yardage is based on 43"/44"
(109 cm/112 cm) wide fabric.

1$\frac{1}{2}$ yds (1.4 m) of black large print fabric

1 yd (91 cm) of black small print fabric

1$\frac{1}{4}$ yds (1.1 m) of white small print fabric

You will also need:

22" (56 cm) two-slider hand bag zipper

$\frac{7}{8}$ yd (80 cm) of fusible fleece (45" [114 cm] wide)

1$\frac{3}{4}$ yds (1.6 m) of medium-weight fusible interfacing (20" [51 cm] wide)

Four 1$\frac{1}{4}$" (32 mm) D-rings

$\frac{5}{8}$ yd (57 cm) of $\frac{3}{8}$" (10 mm) wide elastic

CUTTING OUT THE PIECES

All measurements include $\frac{1}{4}$" seam allowances. Outside pocket pattern is on page 69.

From black large print fabric:

- Cut 2 **front/backs** 14" x 14".
- Cut 1 **daypack flap** 11" x 8".
- Cut 1 **outside pocket** from pattern.
- Cut 1 **outside pocket flap** 10" x 3".
- Cut 1 **outside pocket flap lining** 10" x 3".
- Cut 4 **straps** 4" x 20".
- Cut 2 **zipper facings** 3" x 23".
- Cut 1 **side/bottom** 5$\frac{1}{2}$" x 31".
- Cut 2 **seam binding strips** 2" x 7".

From black small print fabric:
- Cut 3 **seam binding strips** 2" x 40".
- Cut 2 **bottle pockets** 9" x 8".
- Cut 2 **organizer pockets** 14" x 12".
- Cut 1 **daypack flap lining** 11" x 8".

From white small print fabric:
- Cut 2 **front/back linings** 14" x 14".
- Cut 1 **outside pocket lining** from pattern.
- Cut 1 **bottom lining** $5^1/_2$" x $13^1/_2$".
- Cut 2 **side linings** $5^1/_2$" x $9^1/_4$".
- Cut 2 **zipper facing linings** $2^7/_8$" x 23".
- Cut two 2" wide **bias binding strips**, 30" long and 18" long, pieced as needed.

From fusible fleece:
- Cut 2 **front/back fleeces** 14" x 14".
- Cut 4 **strap fleeces** 3" x 18".
- Cut 1 **daypack flap fleece** 11" x 8".

From medium-weight fusible interfacing:
- Cut 1 **side/bottom interfacing** $5^1/_2$" x 31".
- Cut 2 **zipper facing interfacings** 3" x 23".
- Cut 2 **organizer pocket interfacings** 14" x 12".

MAKING THE STRAPS

Follow Sewing and Pressing, page 73, to make daypack. Use a $^1/_4$" seam allowance throughout.

1. Following manufacturer's instructions, center and fuse 1 **strap fleece** on wrong side of each **strap**.
2. Press 1 short edge and then both long edges of each strap $^1/_2$" to wrong side (**Fig. 1**).

Fig. 1

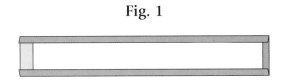

3. Matching wrong sides and long edges, press each strap in half. Topstitch along folded edges and $^1/_4$" from folded edges (**Fig. 2**).

Fig. 2

MAKING THE FRONT/BACK LININGS

1. Following manufacturer's instructions, fuse 1 **organizer pocket interfacing** to wrong side of each **organizer pocket**. Matching wrong sides and long raw edges, press organizer pocket in half. Topstitch along folded edge and $^1/_4$" from folded edge. Repeat with remaining organizer pocket.

2. Matching raw edges, baste organizer pocket to right side of **front lining** along sides and bottom edges of pocket. Stitch divider line in pocket as shown (**Fig. 3**) or as desired. Repeat to sew remaining organizer pocket to **back lining**.

Fig. 3

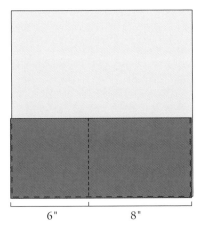

6"   8"

MAKING THE SIDE/BOTTOM LININGS

1. For elastic casing, press 1 long (top) edge of 1 **bottle pocket** $^1/_4$" to wrong side and then press $^5/_8$" to wrong side. Topstitch along bottom edge of casing (**Fig. 4**).

Fig. 4

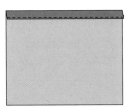

2. Cut a 6" length of elastic. Attach a safety pin to 1 end of elastic; insert elastic into casing. Stitch over both ends of casing to hold elastic in place. Repeat with remaining bottle pocket.

3. Baste $1/8$" and $1/4$" from bottom edge of each bottle pocket for gathering (**Fig. 5**).

Fig. 5

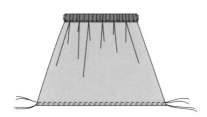

4. Matching right sides and gathering basting threads to fit 1 short edge of **bottom lining**, sew 1 bottle pocket to bottom lining (**Fig. 6**). Sew remaining bottle pocket to opposite short edge of bottom lining.

Fig. 6

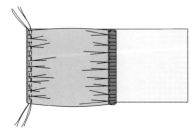

5. Matching right sides and short edges, sew 1 **side lining** to bottom lining (with pocket in between) (**Fig. 7**). Sew remaining side lining to opposite edge of bottom lining.

Fig. 7

6. Baste side edges of bottle pockets to side edges of side linings (**Fig. 8**).

Fig. 8

MAKING THE OUTSIDE POCKET

1. Matching right sides and leaving an opening for turning along top edge, sew **outside pocket** and **outside pocket lining** together along all edges. Turn pocket right side out; stitch opening closed.

2. To make elastic casing, press top edge of outside pocket $1/4$" to lining side and then press $5/8$" to lining side. Topstitch along bottom edge of casing.

3. Cut a $7^1/2$" length of elastic. Attach a safety pin to 1 end of elastic; insert elastic into casing. Stitch over both ends of casing to hold elastic in place (**Fig 9**).

Fig. 9

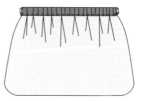

MAKING THE OUTSIDE POCKET FLAP

1. Matching right sides, sew **outside pocket flap** and **outside pocket flap lining** together along 1 long (top) edge. Turn flap right side out; press. Baste layers together around raw edges.

2. To round corners of outside pocket flap, place a drinking glass or lid, approximately $2^1/8$" in diameter, on one bottom corner of flap and draw around glass or lid (**Fig. 10**); trim along drawn line. Repeat for remaining bottom corner.

Fig. 10

3. Matching wrong sides and long raw edges, press the 18" **bias binding strip** in half.
4. Follow **Attaching Closed End Binding**, page 78, to bind side and bottom edges of outside pocket flap (**Fig. 11**).

Fig. 11

MAKING THE ZIPPER ASSEMBLY

Use zipper foot to make zipper assembly.

1. Following manufacturer's instructions, fuse 1 **zipper facing interfacing** to wrong side of each **zipper facing**.
2. Press 1 long edge of each zipper facing and **zipper facing lining** ¹/₂" to wrong side.
3. Position pressed edge of 1 zipper facing lining, right side up, ¹/₈" from teeth on *wrong* side of zipper tape; pin. Topstitch along folded edge of lining (**Fig. 12**).

Fig. 12

4. Position pressed edge of 1 zipper facing lining, right side up, next to teeth on right side of zipper tape; pin. Topstitch along folded edge of lining (**Fig. 13**).

Fig. 13

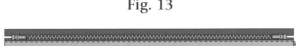

5. Baste long raw edges of zipper facing and zipper facing lining together.
6. Repeat **Steps 3–5** to sew remaining zipper facing and zipper facing lining to remaining zipper tape (**Fig. 14**).

Fig. 14

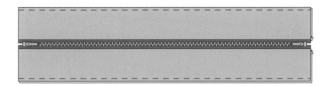

7. If necessary, trim zipper assembly to 5¹/₂" x 23".

MAKING THE FRONT AND BACK

1. Following manufacturer's instructions, fuse 1 **front/back fleece** to wrong side of each **front/back**.
2. Follow **Quilting**, page 75, to quilt front and back as desired. Daypack shown was crosshatch quilted on the diagonal with double lines approximately 1¹/₂" apart.
3. With right sides facing up, pin outside pocket to front 1" above 1 (bottom) edge. Stitch pocket to front along side and bottom edges of pocket and ¹/₄" from side and bottom edges (**Fig. 15**).

Fig. 15

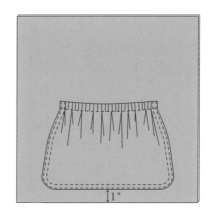

4. With right sides facing and straight long edge of flap centered above top of pocket, stitch outside pocket flap to front along long straight edge of flap (**Fig. 16**). Fold flap over to cover top of pocket.

Fig. 16

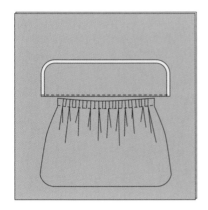

5. Matching wrong sides and stitching around all raw edges, baste **front lining** and front together. Repeat to baste **back lining** and back together.
6. Using a drinking glass or lid with a diameter of approximately 4", round each corner of **front** and **back** in the same manner as corners on outside pocket flap (**Fig. 17**).

Fig. 17

MAKING THE SIDE/BOTTOM
1. Fuse **side/bottom interfacing** to wrong side of **side/bottom**.
2. Matching wrong sides and stitching around all raw edges, baste **side/bottom** and **side/bottom lining** together.

MAKING THE DAYPACK FLAP
1. Fuse **daypack flap fleece** to wrong side of **daypack flap**.
2. Matching wrong sides and stitching around all raw edges, baste **daypack flap lining** and daypack flap together.
3. Follow **Quilting**, page 75, to quilt as desired. Flap shown was crosshatch quilted on the diagonal with double lines $1^1/_2$" apart.

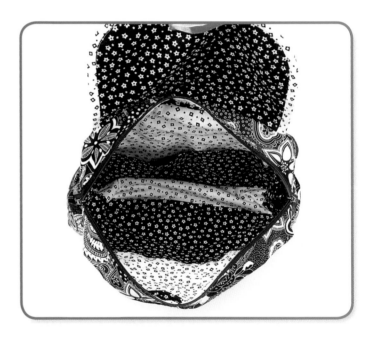

4. Using the 4" diameter drinking glass or lid, round bottom corners of daypack flap (**Fig. 18**).

Fig. 18

5. Matching wrong sides and long edges, press the 30" **bias binding strip** in half.
6. Follow **Attaching Open End Binding**, page 78, to bind side and bottom (curved) edges of daypack flap (**Fig. 19**).

Fig. 19

ASSEMBLING THE DAYPACK

1. Matching right sides and raw edges, sew 1 **strap** to **side/bottom** ³/₄" above bottom edge of each bottle pocket (**Fig. 20**).

Fig. 20

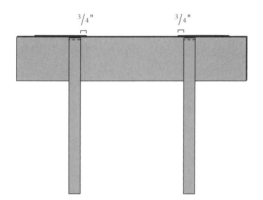

2. Find and mark center of daypack flap and zipper assembly with pins. Matching centers and lining side of flap and right side of zipper assembly, baste flap to zipper assembly (**Fig. 21**).

Fig. 21

3. Matching right sides and raw edges, baste remaining straps to daypack flap 2¹/₄" from sides of flap (**Fig. 22**).

Fig. 22

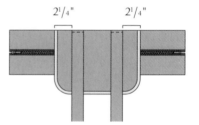

4. Matching right sides and with straps on same edge, sew **zipper assembly** to **side/bottom** (**Fig. 23**).

Fig. 23

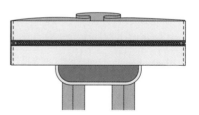

5. Matching wrong sides and long raw edges, press black large print **seam binding strips** in half.
6. Follow **Attaching Open End Binding**, page 78, to bind seam allowances between zipper assembly and side/bottom.

7. Make two $1/2$" tucks in side/bottom as shown (**Fig. 24**). Baste tucks in place along raw edges.

Fig. 24

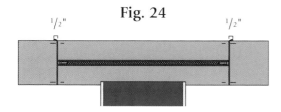

8. Find and mark center top and bottom on both edges of zipper assembly/side/bottom. Mark center top and bottom of **front** and **back**.

9. Aligning centers and matching right sides and raw edges, pin front and zipper assembly/side/bottom together. Pin straps out of the way as needed. Sew front and zipper assembly/side/bottom together. Repeat to sew back and zipper assembly/side/bottom together (**Fig. 25**).

Fig. 25

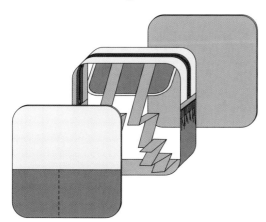

10. Using diagonal seams (**Fig. 26**), sew the 3 black small print **seam binding strips** together to make 1 continuous seam binding strip. Matching wrong sides and long raw edges, press seam binding strip in half.

Fig. 26

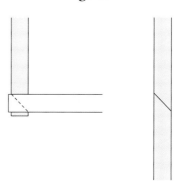

11. Follow **Attaching Continuous Binding**, page 77, to bind raw seam allowances on inside of daypack.

My Soft Ball

Finished Ball Size: 8" (20 cm) diameter

Tips:
You'll be using quite a bit of fiberfill to stuff the ball. You may need to use a small wooden dowel to "poke" fiberfill into the ball.

Different textures stimulate baby's sense of touch. Use as many different "feels" of ribbon and fabric as you wish!

YARDAGE REQUIREMENTS

Scrap or ¹/₄ yd (23 cm) *each* of black print, red print, and white print fabrics

Scrap or ¹/₄ yd (23 cm) *each* of black, red, and white Dot Minkee™ fabrics

You will also need:

Twelve 2¹/₂" (65 mm) long assorted ribbons

Polyester fiberfill

Chalk pencil or water-soluble pen

CUTTING OUT THE PIECES

Ball side pattern is on page 70. When cutting sides, transfer dots on pattern to wrong side of fabric pieces using chalk pencil or water-soluble pen.

From *each* black print, red print, and white print fabric:

• Cut 1 **side** from pattern.

From *each* black, red, and white Dot Minkee fabric:

• Cut 1 **side** from pattern.

MAKING THE BALL

Follow Sewing and Pressing, page 73, to make ball. Use a ¹/₄" seam allowance throughout.

1. Matching wrong sides and ends, fold ribbons in half. Placing as desired and matching raw edges, pin 2 ribbons to 1 edge of each **side**. Sew ribbons in place ¹/₈" from raw edges; backstitch over ribbons to firmly secure.

2. Matching right sides and dots, sew 3 **sides** together to make half of ball. Repeat to sew the remaining 3 sides together.

3. Matching right sides and leaving an opening for turning in 1 seam, sew 2 halves together; turn.

4. Stuff ball firmly with fiberfill. Sew opening closed.

My Soft Blocks

Finished Block Size: 4¹/₂" x 4¹/₂" x 4¹/₂"
(11 cm x 11 cm x 11 cm)

Tips:

To speed things up, use novelty prints instead of appliquéd squares to make blocks.

Use a walking foot to appliqué shapes to Minkee™ and use 2 layers of stabilizer to minimize stretch.

Test appliqué stitch length and width on fabric scraps to achieve desired look.

YARDAGE REQUIREMENTS

*Yardage is based on 43"/44"
(109 cm/112 cm) wide fabric.*

Scraps of assorted black print, red print, and white print fabrics
Scrap or ¹/₄ yd (23 cm) *each* of black, red, and white Dot Minkee™ fabrics
You will also need:
¹/₄ yd (23 cm) of paper-backed fusible web (17" [43 cm] wide)
Stabilizer

CUTTING OUT THE PIECES

All measurements include ¹/₄" seam allowances.

From *each* of 1 black print, 1 red print, and 1 white print fabric:
- Cut 3 **squares** 5" x 5".

From *each* black, red, and white Dot Minkee™ fabric:
- Cut 3 **squares** 5" x 5".

ADDING THE APPLIQUÉS

*Patterns are on pages 67–68. Each block has
3 appliqués: 1 number, 1 letter, and 1 shape.*

1. Trace each appliqué pattern onto paper side
    of fusible web with a pencil, leaving at least
    a $1/2$" space between shapes. Rough cut
    shapes apart; *do not* cut on drawn lines.
2. Following manufacturer's instructions, fuse
    each web shape to wrong side of desired
    print fabric. Carefully cut out shapes along
    drawn lines.
3. Remove paper from back of shapes. Center
    and fuse 1 shape to right side of each Dot
    Minkee™ **square**. *Note: When fusing appliqués
    to Minkee, press from wrong side of fabric or use
    a pressing cloth.*
4. Follow **Machine Appliqué**, page 74, to
    appliqué shapes.

MAKING THE BLOCKS

*Follow **Sewing** and **Pressing**, page 73, to make blocks.
Match right sides and use a $1/4$" seam allowance
throughout.*

1. For each block, select 1 black, 1 red, and
    1 white Dot Minkee™ square and 1 black,
    1 red, and 1 white print fabric square.

2. Arranging **squares** as desired, sew A, B, C,
    and D together. Sew E to the top edge and
    F to the bottom edge of B (**Fig. 1**).

Fig. 1

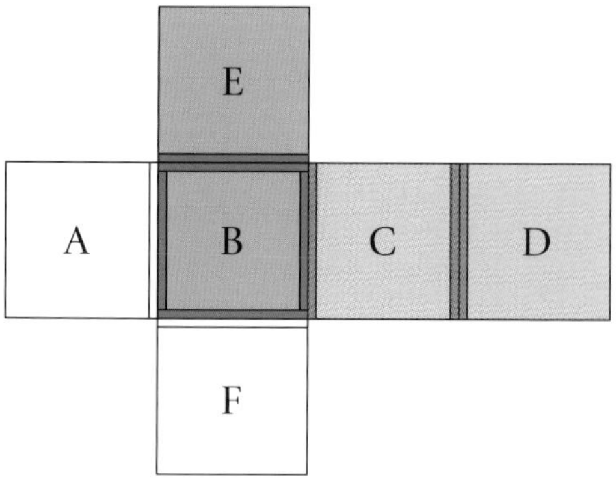

3. Sew A and E, then A and F together. Sew
    E and C, then F and C together. Fold D over
    to make the block shape; pin. Leaving an
    opening for turning and stuffing, sew D to A,
    E and F.
4. Stuff block with fiberfill until firm. Sew
    opening closed.
5. Repeat **Steps 1–4** to make remaining blocks.

Play Date Blankie

Finished Blankie Size: 14" x 14"
(36 cm x 36 cm)

> *Tips:*
> *Use a contrasting color (stretch terry or woven fabric) on back of blankie to change the look.*
> *Use a walking foot to assemble the blankie to reduce slippage and stretching.*

YARDAGE REQUIREMENTS

Yardage is based on 43"/44" (109 cm/112 cm) wide fabric.

- Four 5" x 5" (13 cm x 13 cm) **squares** of assorted red, black, and white print fabrics
- $1/2$ yd (46 cm) of white Dot Minkee™ fabric

You will also need:

- $1^1/8$ yds (1.1 m) of red medium rickrack
- 1 yd (91 cm) of $3/8$" (1 cm) wide black dot grosgrain ribbon
- $1^3/4$ yds (1.6 m) of 1" (25 mm) wide white satin ribbon

CUTTING OUT THE PIECES

All measurements include $1/4$" seam allowances.

From white Dot Minkee™ fabric:

- Cut 1 **backing** $14^1/2$" x $14^1/2$".
- Cut 2 **top/bottom borders** 3" x $9^1/2$".
- Cut 2 **side borders** 3" x $14^1/2$".

MAKING THE BLANKIE

*Follow **Sewing** and **Pressing**, page 73, to assemble blankie. Match right sides and use a $1/4$" seam allowance throughout. Measurements provided include outer seam allowances.*

1. Sew 2 **squares** together to make **Unit 1**. Make 2 Unit 1's.

Unit 1 (make 2)

2. Sew 2 Unit 1's together to make **Four Patch**. Four Patch should measure $9^1/_2$" x $9^1/_2$".

Four Patch

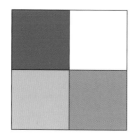

3. Sew 2 **top/bottom borders** to **Four Patch**.
4. Sew 2 **side borders** to **Four Patch** to make blankie top. Blankie top should measure $14^1/_2$" x $14^1/_2$".

Blankie Top

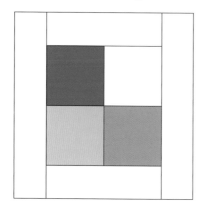

5. From rickrack, cut four $8^3/_4$" lengths. With points of rickrack approximately $1/_{16}$" from seam, center and baste 1 rickrack length on each side of Four Patch (**Fig. 1**). *Note: Since ribbon and rickrack widths vary, you may need to adjust placement of rickrack to allow points of rickrack to show.*

Fig. 1

6. Aligning grosgrain ribbon edge along seams between Four Patch and borders and mitering corners, pin ribbon to Four Patch. Fold end of ribbon $1/_4$" to wrong side and overlap beginning of ribbon $1/_2$". Topstitch in place along long edges of ribbon (**Fig. 2**).

Fig. 2

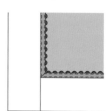

7. Aligning satin ribbon with outer edges of blankie top and mitering corners, pin ribbon to blankie top. Fold end of ribbon $1/_4$" to wrong side and overlap beginning of ribbon $1/_2$". Baste ribbon in place (**Fig. 3**).

Fig. 3

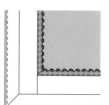

8. Leaving an opening for turning, sew blankie top and backing together. Turn blankie right side out and stitch opening closed. Topstitch along edges of satin ribbon and in the ditch along the seams between the Four Patch and borders. Remove any visible basting.

You're Invited

Shower the new kid with this fun assortment of gifts (Mom will love them, too). The quilt, bib, receiving blanket, and capacious diaper tote are not only invaluable, they make it clear that an important little gal or guy is about to brighten the world with one-of-a-kind style!

Star Baby Quilt

Finished Quilt Size: 51" x 51"
(130 cm x 130 cm)
Finished Small Block Size: 8" x 8"
(20 cm x 20 cm)
Finished Large Block Size: 32" x 32"
(81 cm x 81 cm)

Tip:
Make a test Small Star Block before you start for practice and to make sure your seam allowance is exactly $^1/_4$". And you can use your test Block to make the Receiving Blanket on page 55!

YARDAGE REQUIREMENTS
Yardage is based on 43"/44" (109 cm/112 cm) wide fabric.

   $^7/_8$ yd (80 cm) of alphabet print fabric
   $1^3/_8$ yds (1.3 m) of blue print fabric
   $^1/_4$ yd (23 cm) of blue dot fabric
   $1^3/_8$ yds (1.3 m) of pink dot fabric
   $^3/_8$ yd (34 cm) of green print fabric
   $^5/_8$ yd (57 cm) of green stripe fabric
   $^1/_2$ yd (46 cm) of fabric for binding
   $3^3/_8$ yds (3.1 m) of fabric for backing

You will also need:
   59" x 59" (150 cm x 150 cm) piece of batting

CUTTING OUT THE PIECES
*Follow **Rotary Cutting**, page 72, to cut fabric. All strips are cut across the width of the fabric unless otherwise noted. Borders are cut exact length. All measurements include $^1/_4$" seam allowances.*

From alphabet print fabric:
- Cut 1 strip $8^1/_2$"w. From this strip, cut 4 **large squares** $8^1/_2$" x $8^1/_2$".
- Cut 1 strip $2^1/_2$"w. From this strip, cut 16 **small squares** $2^1/_2$" x $2^1/_2$".

- Cut 1 strip $17^1/_4$"w. From this strip, cut 1 square $17^1/_4$" x $17^1/_4$". Cut square *twice* diagonally to make 4 **large background triangles**.

From remainder of strip:
  - Cut 1 strip $5^1/_4$"w. From this strip, cut 4 squares $5^1/_4$" x $5^1/_4$". Cut squares *twice* diagonally to make 16 **small background triangles**.
  - Cut 3 strips $2^7/_8$"w. From these strips, cut 16 squares $2^7/_8$" x $2^7/_8$". Cut squares *once* diagonally to make 32 **small star point triangles**.

From blue print fabric:
- Cut 2 *lengthwise* **top/bottom outer borders** $4^1/_2$" x $42^1/_2$".

From remainder of width:
  - Cut 1 strip $2^1/_2$"w. From this strip, cut 8 **small squares** $2^1/_2$" x $2^1/_2$".
  - Cut 1 strip $5^1/_4$"w. From this strip, cut 2 squares $5^1/_4$" x $5^1/_4$". Cut squares *twice* diagonally to make 8 **small background triangles**.
  - Cut 2 strips $8^7/_8$"w. From these strips, cut 4 squares $8^7/_8$" x $8^7/_8$". Cut squares *once* diagonally to make 8 **large star point triangles**.
  - Cut 1 strip $2^7/_8$"w. From this strip, cut 8 squares $2^7/_8$" x $2^7/_8$". Cut squares *once* diagonally to make 16 **small star point triangles**.

From blue dot fabric:
- Cut 1 strip $2^1/_2$"w. From this strip, cut 12 **small squares** $2^1/_2$" x $2^1/_2$".
- Cut 1 strip $2^7/_8$"w. From this strip, cut 8 squares $2^7/_8$" x $2^7/_8$". Cut squares *once* diagonally to make 16 **small star point triangles**.

From pink dot fabric:
- Cut 2 *lengthwise* **side outer borders** $4^1/_2$" x $42^1/_2$".

From remainder of width:
  - Cut 1 strip $4^1/_2$"w. From this strip, cut 6 **medium squares** $4^1/_2$" x $4^1/_2$".
  - Cut 2 strips $2^1/_2$"w. From these strips, cut 16 **small squares** $2^1/_2$" x $2^1/_2$".
  - Cut 1 square $9^1/_4$" x $9^1/_4$". Cut square *twice* diagonally to make 4 **medium background triangles**.
  - Cut 1 strip $5^1/_4$"w. From this strip, cut 4 squares $5^1/_4$" x $5^1/_4$". Cut squares *twice* diagonally to make 16 **small background triangles**.

From green print fabric:
- Cut 1 strip $4^7/_8$"w. From these strips, cut 4 squares $4^7/_8$" x $4^7/_8$". Cut squares *once* diagonally to make 8 **medium star point triangles**.
- Cut 1 strip $2^7/_8$"w. From this strip, cut 8 squares $2^7/_8$" x $2^7/_8$". Cut squares *once* diagonally to make 16 **small star point triangles**.
- Cut 1 strip $4^1/_2$"w. From this strip, cut 2 **medium squares** $4^1/_2$" x $4^1/_2$".

From remainder of strip:
  - Cut 1 strip $2^1/_2$"w. From this strip, cut 12 **small squares** $2^1/_2$" x $2^1/_2$".

From green stripe fabric:
- Cut 2 **side inner borders** $1^1/_2$" x $40^1/_2$", pieced as needed.
- Cut 2 **top/bottom inner borders** $1^1/_2$" x $42^1/_2$", pieced as needed.
- Cut 4 **flange strips** 1" x $50^1/_2$", pieced as needed.
- Cut 1 strip $4^1/_2$"w. From this strip, cut 4 **medium squares** $4^1/_2$" x $4^1/_2$".

From fabric for binding:
- Cut 6 **binding strips** $2^1/_2$"w.

MAKING THE SMALL BLOCKS

*Follow **Sewing** and **Pressing**, page 73, to assemble the quilt top. Use a ¹/₄" seam allowance throughout. Measurements provided include outer seam allowances.*

1. Sew 1 blue dot **small square** and 1 green print **small square** together to make **Unit 1**. Press seam allowances to green print fabric. Make 2 **Unit 1's**.

Unit 1 (make 2)

2. Sew 2 **Unit 1's** together to make **Four Patch**. Four Patch should measure 4¹/₂" x 4¹/₂".

Four Patch

3. Matching triangle points as shown by arrows in **Fig. 1**, sew 2 blue dot **small star point triangles** and 1 alphabet print **small background triangle** together to make **Small Flying Geese**. Press seam allowances to star point triangles. Small Flying Geese should measure 4¹/₂" x 2¹/₂". Make 4 Small Flying Geese.

Fig. 1

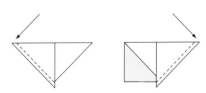

Small Flying Geese (make 4)

4. Sew 1 **Small Flying Geese** and 2 alphabet print **small squares** together to make **Unit 2**. Press seam allowances to squares. Make 2 Unit 2's.

Unit 2 (make 2)

5. Sew 2 **Flying Geese** and **Four Patch** together to make **Unit 3**. Press seam allowances to Four Patch.

Unit 3

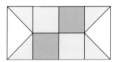

6. Sew 2 **Unit 2's** and **Unit 3** together to make **Block A**. Press seam allowances to Unit 3. Block A should measure 8¹/₂" x 8¹/₂".

7. Repeat **Steps 1–6** to make a total of 2 Block A's.

Block A (make 2)

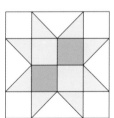

8. Using 1 green stripe **medium square** (in place of Four Patch), 8 alphabet print **small star point triangles**, 4 pink dot **small squares** and 4 pink dot **small background triangles**, repeat **Steps 3–6** to make **Block B**. Block B should measure 8¹/₂" x 8¹/₂". Make 4 Block B's.

9. Using 1 green print **medium square** (in place of Four Patch), 8 blue print **small star point triangles**, 4 alphabet print **small squares** and 4 alphabet print **small background triangles**, repeat **Steps 3–6** to make **Block C**. Block C should measure 8¹/₂" x 8¹/₂". Make 2 Block C's.

Block B (make 4)

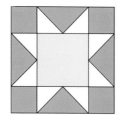

Block C (make 2)

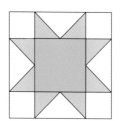

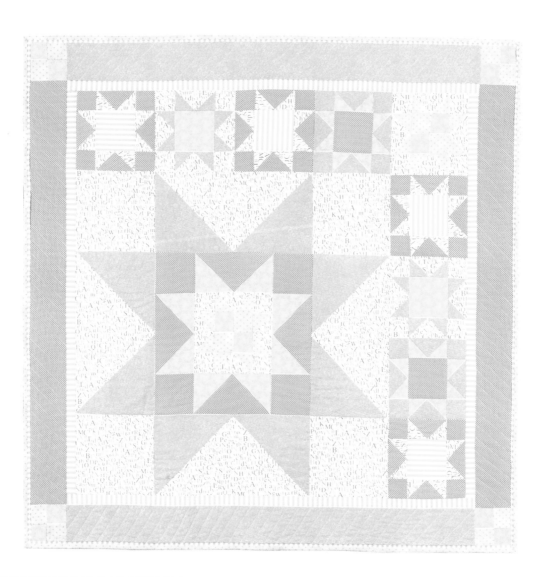

10. Using 1 pink dot **medium square** (in place of Four Patch), 8 green print **small star point triangles**, 4 blue print **small squares** and 4 blue print **small background triangles**, repeat **Steps 3–6** to make **Block D**. Block D should measure 8¹/₂" x 8¹/₂". Make 2 Block D's.

Block D (make 2)

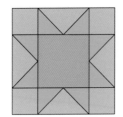

MAKING THE LARGE BLOCK

1. In the same manner as Small Flying Geese and using green print **medium star point triangles** and pink dot **medium background triangles**, make 4 **Medium Flying Geese**. Medium Flying Geese should measure 8¹/₂" x 4¹/₂".

Medium Flying Geese (make 4)

2. Sew 1 **Medium Flying Geese** and 2 pink dot **medium squares** together to make **Unit 4**. Press seam allowances to squares. Make 2 Unit 4's.

Unit 4 (make 2)

3. Sew 2 **Medium Flying Geese** and 1 **Block A** together to make **Unit 5**. Press seam allowances to Block A.

Unit 5

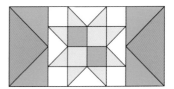

4. Sew 2 **Unit 4's** and **Unit 5** together to make **Unit 6**. Press seam allowances to Unit 5. Unit 6 should measure 16¹/₂" x 16¹/₂".

Unit 6

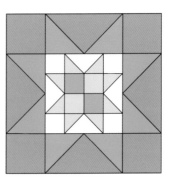

5. In the same manner as Small Flying Geese and using blue print **large star point triangles** and alphabet print **large background triangles**, make 4 **Large Flying Geese**. Large Flying Geese should measure 16¹/₂" x 8¹/₂".

Large Flying Geese (make 4)

6. Sew 1 **Large Flying Geese** and 2 alphabet print **large squares** together to make **Unit 7**. Press seam allowances to large squares. Make 2 Unit 7's.

Unit 7 (make 2)

7. Sew 2 **Large Flying Geese** and **Unit 6** together to make **Unit 8**. Press seam allowances to Unit 6.

Unit 8

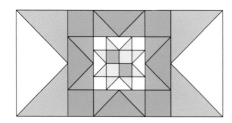

8. Sew 2 **Unit 7's** and **Unit 8** together to make **Large Block**. Press seam allowances to Unit 8. Large Block should measure $32^{1}/_{2}$" x $32^{1}/_{2}$".

Large Block

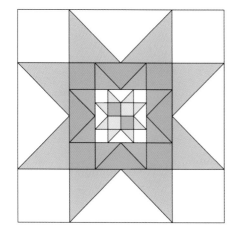

ASSEMBLING THE QUILT TOP CENTER
Refer to Quilt Top Diagram, page 54, for placement.
1. Sew 1 **Block A**, 2 **Block B's**, 1 **Block C**, and 1 **Block D** together to make **Top Row**.
2. Sew 2 **Block B's**, 1 **Block C**, and 1 **Block D** together to make **Unit 9**.

Unit 9

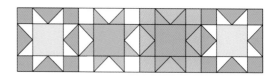

3. Sew **Large Block** and **Unit 9** together to make **Bottom Row**.
4. Sew **Top** and **Bottom Rows** together to make quilt top center.

ADDING THE BORDERS
1. Matching centers and corners, sew **side inner borders** to quilt top center.
2. Matching centers and corners, sew **top/ bottom inner borders** to quilt top center.
3. Matching centers and corners, sew **side outer borders** to quilt top.
4. Sew 1 blue dot **small square** and 1 green print **small square** together to make **Unit 10**. Press seam allowances to green print. Make 8 **Unit 10's**.

Unit 10 (make 8)

5. Sew 2 **Unit 10's** together to make **Corner Four Patch**. Corner Four Patch should measure 4^1/$_2$" x 4^1/$_2$". Make 4 Corner Four Patches.

Corner Four Patch (make 4)

6. Sew 1 **Corner Four Patch** to each end of **top/bottom outer borders**. Matching centers and corners, sew top/bottom outer borders to quilt.

COMPLETING THE QUILT

1. Follow **Quilting**, page 75, to mark, layer, and quilt as desired. Quilt shown was machine quilted in the ditch. The alphabet print areas of the Large Block were meander quilted and the outer borders were channel quilted.

2. Matching wrong sides and long raw edges, press each **flange strip** in half.

3. Aligning raw edges of flange strip with raw edge of quilt top, baste 1 flange strip to each side of quilt, and then to top and bottom of quilt.

4. Using diagonal seams, **Fig. 2**, sew **binding strips** together to make continuous 2^1/$_2$"w straight-grain binding. Matching wrong sides and long raw edges, press binding in half.

Fig. 2

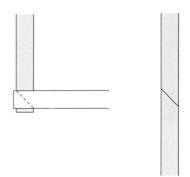

5. Follow **Attaching Binding with Mitered Corners**, page 79, to bind quilt.

Quilt Top Diagram

Receiving Blanket

Finished Blanket Size: 32" x 40" (81 cm x 102 cm)

Tips:

Save time by using a printed flannel; no pieced block required.

Use a lightweight knit or fleece and monogram the baby's initial on the blanket.

Use two packages of extra wide double fold binding instead of making your own.

YARDAGE REQUIREMENTS

Yardage is based on 43"/44" (109 cm/112 cm) wide fabric.

1^1/$_2$ yds (1.4 m) of white cotton flannel

^{3}/$_4$ yd (69 cm) of blue print fabric

6" x 12" (15 cm x 30 cm) piece of pink dot fabric

4" x 13" (10 cm x 33 cm) piece of alphabet print fabric

You will also need:

8^1/$_2$" x 8^1/$_2$" (22 cm x 22 cm) piece of lightweight fusible interfacing

CUTTING OUT THE PIECES

All measurements include ^{1}/$_4$" seam allowances.

From white cotton flannel:

- Cut 1 **blanket** 32" x 40".
- Cut 1 square 9" x 9". Cut square *once* diagonally to make **hood**. (You will use 1 triangle for hood and have 1 left over.)

From blue print fabric:

- Cut 1 **square for binding** 24" x 24".
- Cut 1 **large square** 4^1/$_2$" x 4^1/$_2$".

From pink dot fabric:

- Cut 1 square 5^1/$_4$" x 5^1/$_4$". Cut square *twice* diagonally to make 4 **background triangles**.
- Cut 4 **small squares** 2^1/$_2$" x 2^1/$_2$".

From alphabet print fabric:

- Cut 4 squares 2^7/$_8$" x 2^7/$_8$". Cut squares *once* diagonally to make 8 **star point triangles**.

MAKING THE BLOCK

*Follow **Sewing** and **Pressing**, page 73, to make receiving blanket. Use a ¹/₄" seam allowance throughout. Measurements provided include outer seam allowances.*

1. Using blue print **large square** (in place of Four Patch), 8 alphabet print **star point triangles**, 4 pink dot **small squares**, and 4 pink dot **background triangles**, repeat **Steps 3–6** of **Making the Small Blocks**, page 50, to make **Block**. Block should measure 8¹/₂" x 8¹/₂".

Block

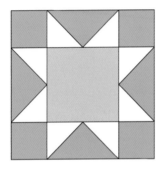

COMPLETING THE RECEIVING BLANKET

1. Matching right side of Block and fusible side of interfacing, sew interfacing to Block along all edges. Carefully cut a slit in center of interfacing; turn Block right side out through slit. Finger press edges so that interfacing is not visible from Block side.
2. Position Block on **blanket** 3" from left and bottom edges of blanket (**Fig. 1**). Following manufacturer's instructions, fuse Block to blanket.

Fig. 1

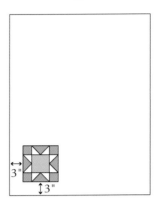

3. Topstitch Block along all edges.
4. Use **square for binding** and follow **Making a Continuous Bias Strip**, page 76, to make approximately 4³/₄ yds of 2¹/₂"w bias binding. Matching wrong sides and long raw edges, press binding in half.
5. From binding, cut a 15" strip. Follow **Attaching Open End Binding**, page 78, to bind long edge of **hood**.
6. With right sides facing up and matching raw edges, pin hood to blanket at corner opposite Block; baste along short edges of hood.
7. To round corners of blanket, place a drinking glass or lid (approximately 4" in diameter) on one corner of blanket and draw around glass or lid (**Fig. 2**); trim along drawn line. Repeat for remaining corners.

Fig. 2

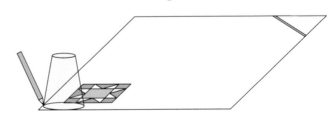

8. Use remaining binding and follow **Attaching Continuous Binding**, page 77, to bind receiving blanket.

Star of the Day Bib

Finished Bib Size: Approximately 11" x 15" (28 cm x 38 cm)

Tips:
Save time by using an 11" x 4¹/₂" piece of novelty print fabric instead of the pieced band.
Use polyester thread for sewing stretch terry.

YARDAGE REQUIREMENTS
Yardage is based on 43"/44" (109 cm/112 cm) wide fabric.

³/₈ yd (34 cm) of white stretch terry knit
¹/₄ yd (23 cm) of alphabet print fabric
¹/₂ yd (46 cm) of green print fabric
Scrap of blue dot fabric

You will also need:

1" (25 mm) length of ³/₄" (19 mm) wide piece of sew-in hook and loop fastener
Stabilizer

CUTTING OUT THE PIECES
All measurements include ¹/₄" seam allowances. Bib pattern is on page 71.

From white stretch terry knit:
- Cut 1 **bib front** from pattern.
- Cut 1 **bib back rectangle** 12" x 16".

From alphabet print fabric:
- Cut 1 **large rectangle** 5¹/₂" x 4¹/₂".
- Cut 1 **small rectangle** 2" x 4¹/₂".
- Cut 1 square 3¹/₄" x 3¹/₄". Cut square *twice* diagonally to make 4 **background triangles**.
- Cut 4 **small squares** 1¹/₂" x 1¹/₂".

From green print fabric:
- Cut two 1¹/₂" wide **bias strips**, 55" long and 20" long, pieced as needed.
- Cut 2 **trim strips** 1" x 11".
- Cut 1 **large square** 2¹/₂" x 2¹/₂".

From blue dot fabric:
- Cut 4 squares 1⁷/₈" x 1⁷/₈". Cut squares *once* diagonally to make 8 **star point triangles**.

MAKING THE BAND

*Follow **Sewing** and **Pressing**, page 73, to make bib. Use a $1/4$" seam allowance throughout. Measurements provided include outer seam allowances.*

1. Matching triangle points as shown by arrows in **Fig. 1**, sew 2 **star point triangles** and 1 **background triangle** together to make **Flying Geese**. Press seam allowances to star point triangles. Flying Geese should measure $2^1/2$" x $1^1/2$". Make 4 Flying Geese.

Fig. 1

Flying Geese (make 4)

2. Sew 1 **Flying Geese** and 2 **small squares** together to make **Unit 1**. Press seam allowances to squares. Make 2 Unit 1's.

Unit 1 (make 2)

3. Sew 2 **Flying Geese** and **large square** together to make **Unit 2**. Press seam allowances to square.

Unit 2

4. Sew 2 **Unit 1's** and **Unit 2** together to make **Block**. Press seam allowances to Unit 2. Block should measure $4^1/2$" x $4^1/2$".

Block

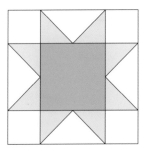

5. Sew **Block**, **small rectangle**, and **large rectangle** together to make **Unit 3**. Press seam allowances to rectangles. Unit 3 should measure 11" x $4^1/2$".

Unit 3

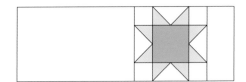

6. Matching wrong sides and long raw edges, press each **trim strip** in half.
7. Matching raw edges, sew **trim strips** to top and bottom edges of **Unit 3** to make **band**. Press seam allowances away from trim strips.

Band

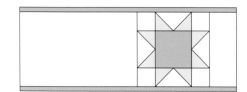

COMPLETING THE BIB

Note: A walking foot may make bib assembly easier.

1. Using a medium length and narrow width zigzag and taking care not to stretch fabric, stitch around **bib front** to stabilize raw edges.
2. Pin stabilizer to wrong side of bib front.
3. With right sides facing up, pin **band** to **bib front** with bottom edge of band 1¹/₄" from bottom edge of bib front. Zigzag along top and bottom edges of each trim strip. Carefully remove stabilizer.
4. Matching wrong sides, center **bib front** on **bib back rectangle**. Stitching along edge of bib front, zigzag bib front and bib back together. Trim bib back even with edges of bib front.
5. Matching wrong sides and long raw edges, press each **bias strip** in half.

6. Using 55" long **bias strip**, follow **Attaching Open End Binding**, page 78, to bind raw outer edges of bib.
7. Using 20" long **bias strip**, follow **Attaching Closed End Binding**, page 78, to bind raw neck edges of bib.
8. Overlap bib closure to determine desired placement of hook and loop fastener pieces (**Fig. 2**). Sew fastener pieces in place.

Fig. 2

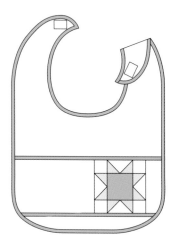

Star Diaper Tote

Finished Tote Size: 18" x 18³/₄" x 4¹/₂"
(46 cm x 48 cm x 11 cm)

Tips:
   Save time by using two 8¹/₂" squares of novelty print fabric instead of the pieced blocks.
   Use webbing instead of making handles.
   Use a sport mesh for the inside pockets and bind with a pretty print fabric.

YARDAGE REQUIREMENTS

Yardage is based on 43"/44" (109 cm/112 cm) wide fabric.
   1¹/₂ yds (1.4 m) of pink dot of fabric
   1⁵/₈ yds (1.5 m) of blue print fabric
   ¹/₈ yd (11 cm) of blue dot fabric
   ³/₄ yd (69 cm) of green print fabric
   ¹/₄ yd (23 cm) of green stripe fabric
   ³/₈ yd (34 cm) of alphabet print fabric
You will also need:
   22" (56 cm) sport-weight zipper
   1¹/₈ yds (1 m) of fusible fleece (45" [114 cm] wide)
   1¹/₄ yds (1.1 m) of Pellon® Decor-Bond® fusible interfacing (45" [114 cm] wide)
   ³/₄ yd (69 cm) of Pellon® Peltex®70 heavy-weight fusible interfacing (20" [51 cm] wide)

CUTTING OUT THE PIECES

All measurements include ¹/₄" seam allowances.
From pink dot fabric:
- Cut 2 **front/backs** 23" x 14".
- Cut 2 **zipper facings** 23" x 3".
- Cut 2 **zipper facing linings** 23" x 2⁷/₈".
- Cut 2 **large inside pockets** 23" x 7¹/₂".
- Cut 2 **large inside pocket linings** 23" x 7¹/₂".
- Cut 4 **top/bottom sashings** 1³/₄" x 11".

From blue print fabric:
- Cut 1 **body lining** 23" x 42".
- Cut 2 **handles** 3³/₄" x 42", pieced as needed.
- Cut 2 **seam binding strips** 1¹/₂" x 22".
- Cut 2 **outside pocket linings** 11" x 11".

From blue dot fabric:
- Cut 8 squares 2⁷/₈" x 2⁷/₈". Cut squares *once* diagonally to make 16 **star point triangles**.

From green print fabric:
- Cut 1 **bottom** 23" x 15".
- Cut 2 **large squares** $4^1/2$" x $4^1/2$".
- Cut 2 **trim strips** 2" x 23".

From green stripe fabric:
- Cut 3 **binding strips** $2^1/2$"w. Cut 1 of these strips into 2 binding strips 12" long and 2 binding strips 6" long.

From alphabet print fabric:
- Cut 1 **small inside pocket** 11" x 6".
- Cut 1 **small inside pocket lining** 11" x 6".
- Cut 2 squares $5^1/4$" x $5^1/4$". Cut squares *twice* diagonally to make 8 **background triangles**.
- Cut 8 **small squares** $2^1/2$" x $2^1/2$".
- Cut 4 **side sashings** $1^3/4$" x $8^1/2$".

From fusible fleece:
- Cut 1 **body fleece** 23" x 42".
- Cut 2 **outside pocket fleeces** 11" x 11".

From Pellon® Decor-Bond®:
- Cut 1 **body interfacing** 22" x 42".
- Cut 2 **large inside pocket interfacings** 23" x $7^1/2$".
- Cut 1 **small inside pocket interfacing** 11" x 6".

From Pellon® Peltex®70:
- Cut 4 **handle interfacings** $1^1/4$" x 21".
- Cut 1 **bottom interfacing** 17" x 6".

MAKING THE HANDLES

*Follow **Sewing** and **Pressing**, page 73. Match right sides and raw edges and use a $^1/4$" seam allowance unless otherwise indicated.*

1. Cut 2 **handle interfacings** in half to make four $1^1/2$" x $10^1/2$" pieces.
2. Butt ends of 1 long and 2 short interfacing pieces together (**Fig. 1**); zigzag ends together. Repeat with remaining handle interfacings.

Fig. 1

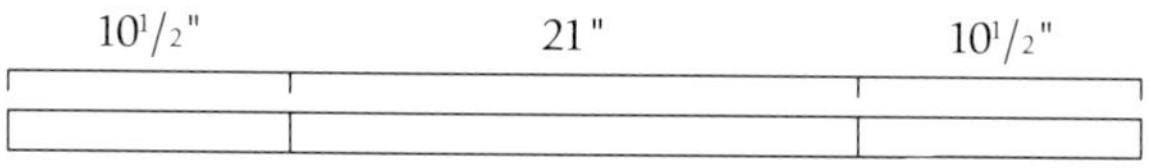

$10^1/2$"   21" $10^1/2$"

3. Press 1 long edge of each **handle** $^3/8$" to the wrong side.
4. Following manufacturer's instructions, fuse 1 handle interfacing to wrong side of 1 handle along unpressed long edge (**Fig. 2**).

Fig. 2

5. Fold interfaced edge over once (**Fig. 3**), then fold pressed edge over interfaced edge (**Fig. 4**).

Fig. 3   **Fig. 4**

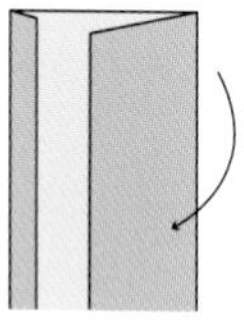

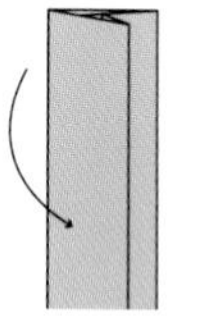

6. Referring to **Fig. 5**, topstitch along folded edge and each long edge of handle.

Fig. 5

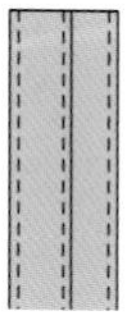

7. Repeat **Steps 4–6** for remaining handle.

MAKING THE OUTSIDE POCKETS

Measurements provided include outer seam allowances.

1. Matching triangle points as shown by arrows in **Fig. 6**, sew 2 **star point triangles** and 1 **background triangle** together to make **Flying Geese**. Press seam allowances to star point triangles. Flying Geese should measure $4^1/_2$" x $2^1/_2$". Make 8 Flying Geese.

Fig. 6

Flying Geese (make 8)

2. Sew 1 **Flying Geese** and 2 **small squares** together to make **Unit 1**. Press seam allowances to squares. Make 4 Unit 1's.

Unit 1 (make 4)

3. Sew 2 **Flying Geese** and 1 **large square** together to make **Unit 2**. Press seam allowances to square. Make 2 Unit 2's.

Unit 2 (make 2)

4. Sew 2 **Unit 1's** and 1 **Unit 2** together to make **Block**. Press seam allowances to Unit 2. Block should measure $8^1/_2$" x $8^1/_2$". Make 2 Blocks.

Block (make 2)

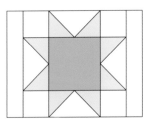

5. Sew **Block** and 2 **side sashings** together to make **Unit 3**. Make 2 Unit 3's.

Unit 3 (make 2)

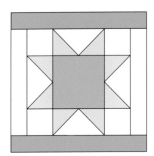

6. Sew **Unit 3** and 2 **top/bottom sashings** together to make **outside pocket**. Outside pocket should measure 11" x 11". Make 2 outside pockets.

Outside Pocket (make 2)

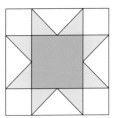

7. Following manufacturer's instructions, fuse 1 **outside pocket fleece** to wrong side of each outside pocket.
8. Matching wrong sides and raw edges, baste 1 outside pocket and 1 **outside pocket lining** together. Repeat with remaining outside pocket and outside pocket lining. Follow **Quilting**, page 75, to quilt pockets, if desired. Pockets shown were quilted in the ditch.
9. Matching wrong sides and long edges, press each 12" **binding strip** in half.
10. Follow **Attaching Open End Binding**, page 78, to bind top edge of each pocket.

MAKING THE INSIDE POCKETS

1. Following manufacturer's instructions, fuse 1 **large inside pocket interfacing** to wrong side of each **large inside pocket**. Fuse **small inside pocket interfacing** to wrong side of **small inside pocket**.
2. Matching right sides and raw edges, sew 1 large inside pocket and 1 **large inside pocket lining** together along long edges.
3. Turn pocket right side out and press. Topstitch along 1 long (top) edge and $^1/_4$" from top edge.
4. Repeat **Steps 2–3** to complete remaining large inside pocket and small inside pocket.

MAKING THE ZIPPER ASSEMBLY

Use zipper foot to make zipper assembly.

1. Press 1 long edge of each **zipper facing** and **zipper facing lining** $^1/_2$" to wrong side.
2. Position pressed edge of 1 zipper facing lining, right side up, $^1/_8$" from teeth on *wrong* side of zipper tape; pin. Topstitch along folded edge of facing (**Fig. 7**).

Fig. 7

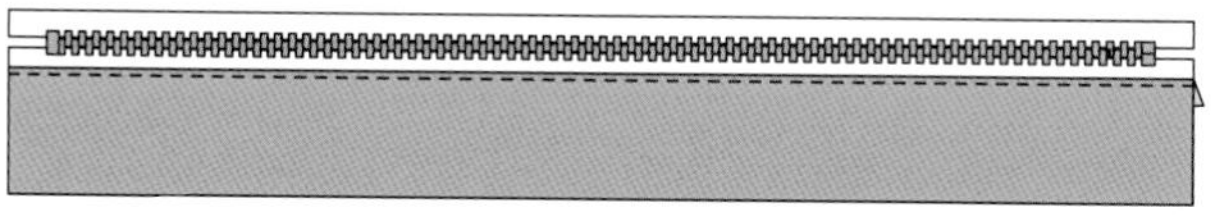

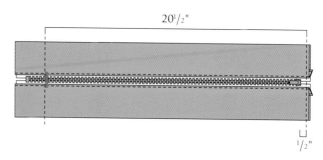

3. Position pressed edge of 1 zipper facing, right side up, next to teeth on right side of zipper tape; pin. Topstitch along folded edge of facing (**Fig. 8**).

Fig. 8

4. Baste long raw edges of zipper facing and zipper facing lining together.
5. Repeat **Steps 2–4** to sew remaining zipper facing and zipper facing lining to opposite zipper tape.
6. Mark 1 cutting line on zipper assembly $^1/_2$" from zipper pull. Mark a second cutting line as shown in **Fig. 9**. Before cutting, stitch across end of zipper several times (shown in blue). Cut on marked lines. Zipper assembly should measure $20^1/_2$" long.

Fig. 9

20$^1/_2$"

$^1/_2$"

7. Matching wrong sides and long edges, press each 6" **binding strip** in half.
8. Follow **Attaching Open End Binding**, page 78, to bind short edges of zipper assembly.

ASSEMBLING THE OUTER TOTE

1. Sew **front**, **back**, and **bottom** together to make **tote body**.

Tote Body

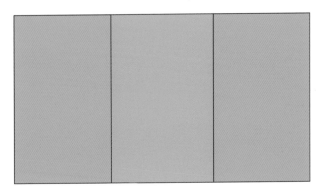

2. Fuse **body fleece** to wrong side of tote body. Stitch in the ditch along seam lines.
3. Aligning bottom edges of outside pockets with seams, center and pin pockets to tote body. Baste sides and bottoms of pockets to tote body (**Fig. 10**).

Fig. 10

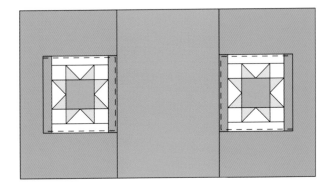

4. Pin handles on sides of pockets, covering side sashings (**Fig. 11**).

Fig. 11

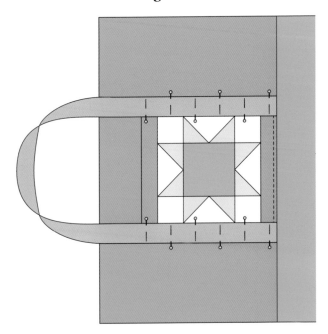

5. Topstitch handles in place, stitching over existing outer topstitching and across handles at top edges of pockets (**Fig. 12**).

Fig. 12

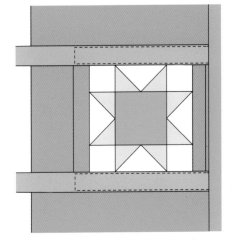

6. Matching wrong sides and long raw edges, press each **trim strip** in half.

7. Position 1 trim strip with long raw edges $^1/_8$" below 1 seam on tote body. Stitch $^1/_4$" from long raw edges of trim strip (**Fig. 13**). Fold and press trim strip over seam, covering raw edges of pocket and strap; topstitch along folded edge. Repeat to sew remaining strip to tote body.

Fig. 13

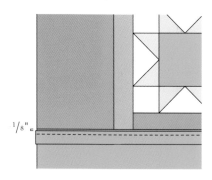

ASSEMBLING THE TOTE LINING

1. Center and fuse **body interfacing** to wrong side of **body lining**.

2. Center and fuse **bottom interfacing** to wrong side of body lining (shown by grey lines in **Fig. 14**). Topstitch along edges of interfacing (**Fig. 14**).

3. Matching raw edges and with right sides facing up, pin 1 large inside pocket 11" from each short edge of body lining. Center and pin small inside pocket $4^1/_2$" from 1 short edge. Baste large inside pockets to lining along side edges of pockets; topstitch along bottom edges. Topstitch small inside pocket to lining along side and bottom edges of pocket. Stitch divider lines in pockets as shown (**Fig. 14**) or as desired.

Fig. 14

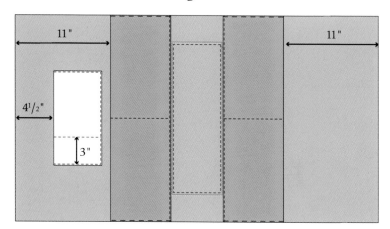

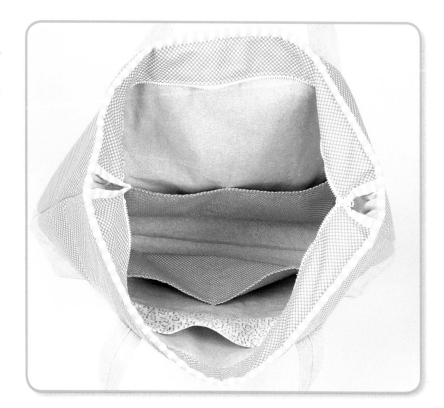

COMPLETING THE TOTE

1. Matching wrong sides and raw edges, layer tote lining and outer tote. Baste layers together around edges.
2. Matching short edges and with lining to outside, fold tote in half. Sew side seams.
3. Matching long edges and wrong sides, fold each **seam binding strip** in half.
4. Follow **Attaching Closed End Binding**, page 78, to bind side seam allowances, closing binding at bottom of seams and trimming binding even with top edge of tote.
5. To box bottom, match right sides and align tote side seams with center of tote bottom. Refer to **Fig. 15** to sew across corner 2¹/₄" from tip. Repeat for remaining side seam and bottom. Fold points toward top of tote and tack to side seam binding. Turn tote right side out.

Fig. 15

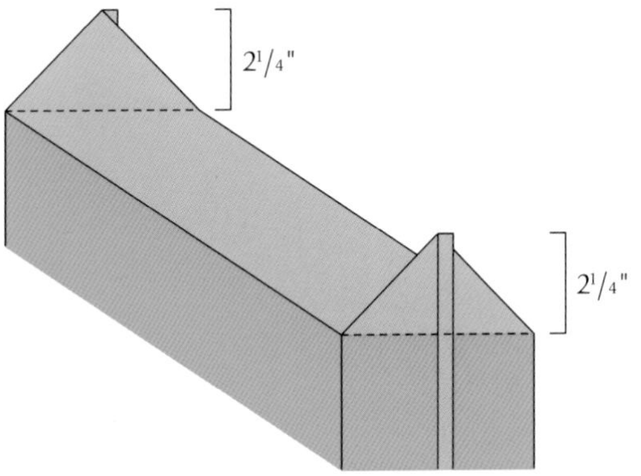

6. Centering zipper assembly and matching wrong sides and raw edges, pin each long side of zipper assembly to tote (**Fig. 16**). Baste zipper assembly to tote front and back.

Fig. 16

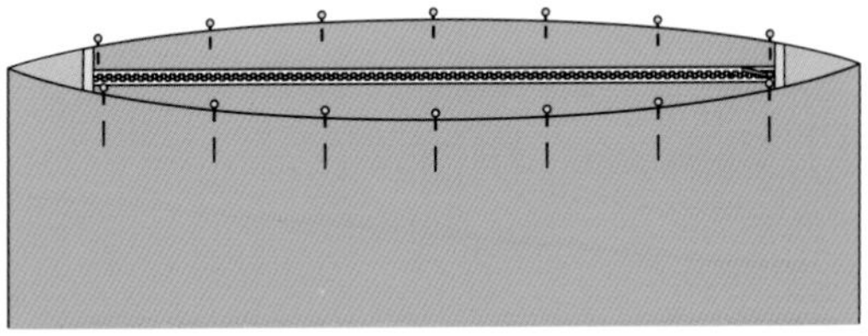

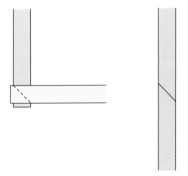

7. Using diagonal seams (**Fig. 17**), sew 2 remaining **binding strips** together end to end to make continuous binding. Trim seam allowances to ¹/₄" and press open.

Fig. 17

8. Matching wrong sides and long raw edges, press binding in half.
9. Follow **Attaching Continuous Binding**, page 77, to bind top of tote.

Appliqué Patterns
for My Soft Blocks,
page 43.

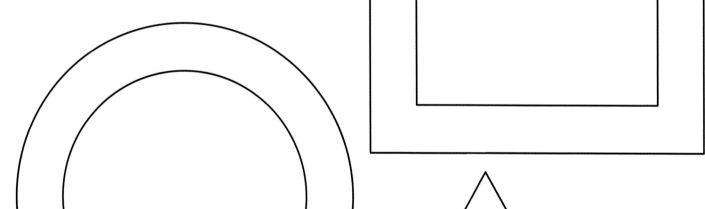

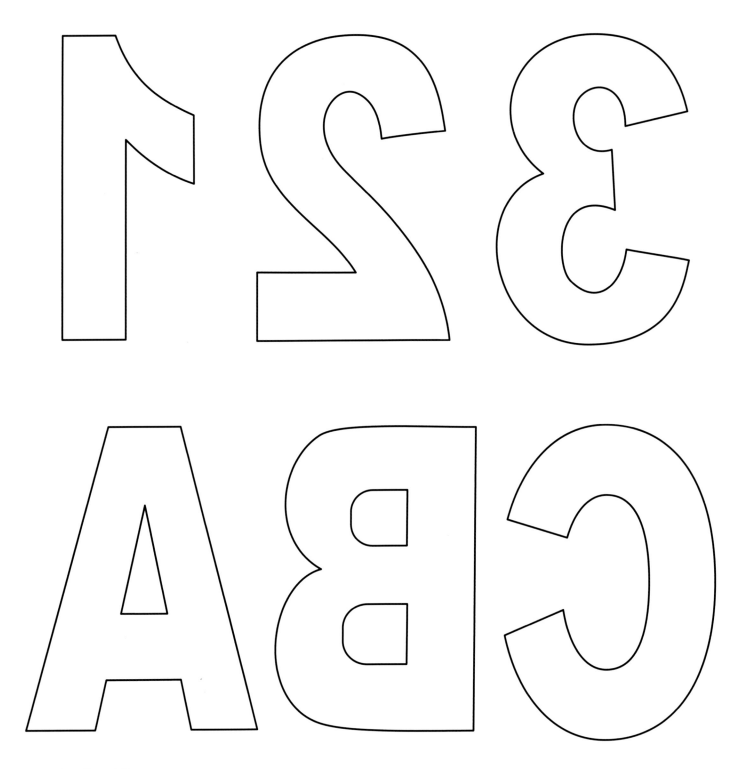

Appliqué Patterns
for My Soft Blocks,
page 43.

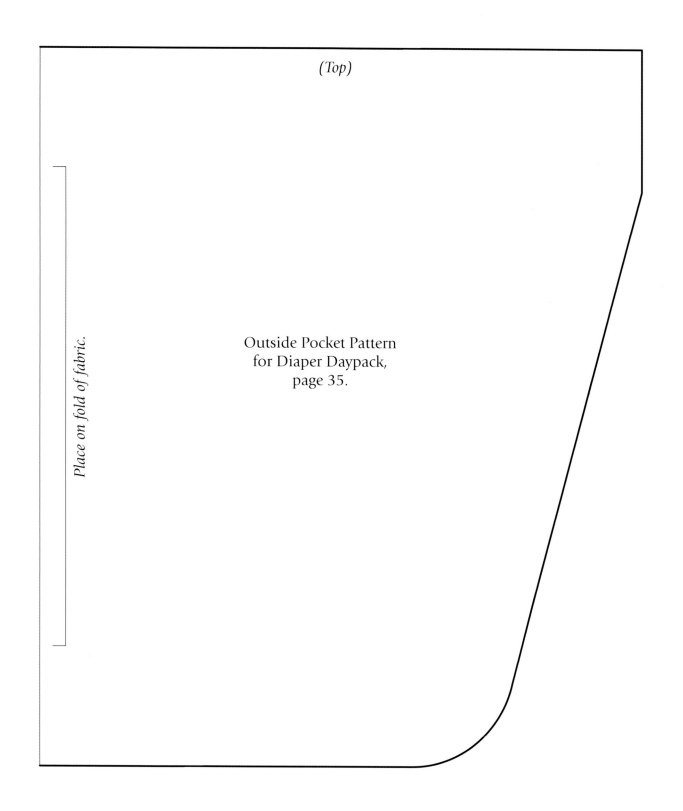

(Top)

Place on fold of fabric.

Outside Pocket Pattern
for Diaper Daypack,
page 35.

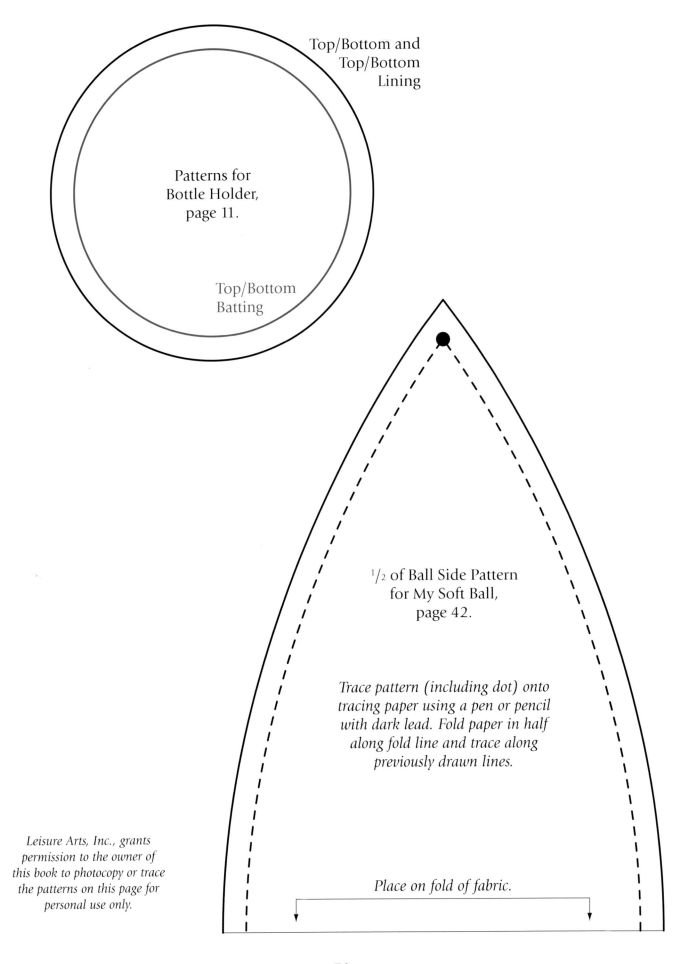

Top/Bottom and
Top/Bottom
Lining

Patterns for
Bottle Holder,
page 11.

Top/Bottom
Batting

¹/₂ of Ball Side Pattern
for My Soft Ball,
page 42.

*Trace pattern (including dot) onto
tracing paper using a pen or pencil
with dark lead. Fold paper in half
along fold line and trace along
previously drawn lines.*

Place on fold of fabric.

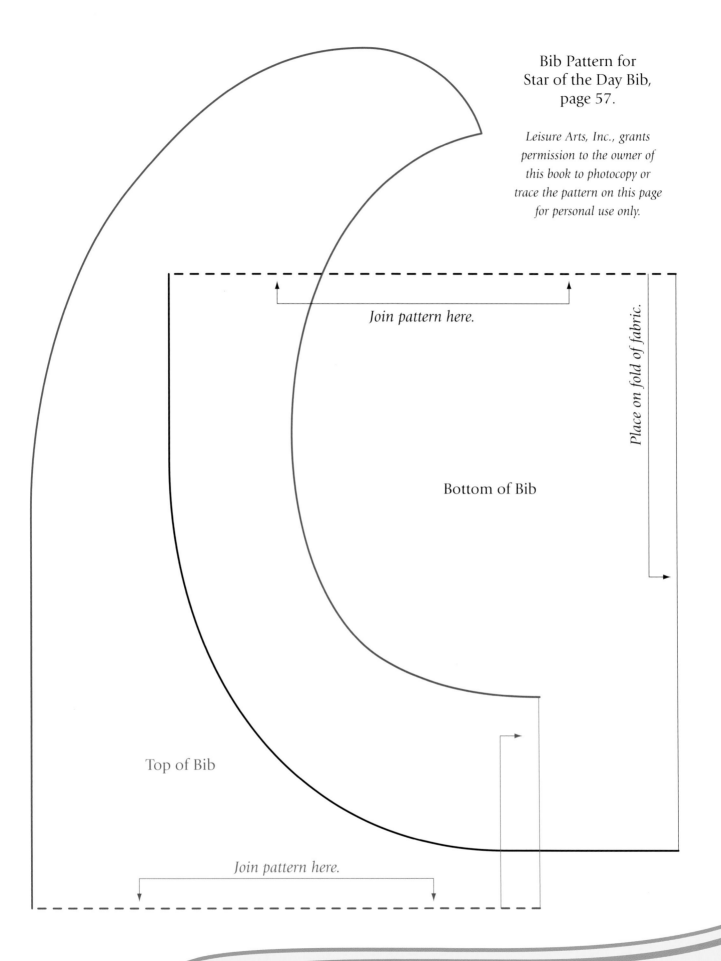

Bib Pattern for
Star of the Day Bib,
page 57.

*Leisure Arts, Inc., grants
permission to the owner of
this book to photocopy or
trace the pattern on this page
for personal use only.*

Join pattern here.

Place on fold of fabric.

Bottom of Bib

Top of Bib

Join pattern here.

General Instructions

To make your sewing easier and more enjoyable, we encourage you to carefully read all of the general instructions, study the color photographs, and familiarize yourself with the individual project instructions before beginning a project.

FABRICS

SELECTING FABRICS
Choose high-quality, medium-weight 100% cotton fabrics. All-cotton fabrics hold a crease better, fray less, and are easier to sew and press than cotton/polyester blends.

Yardage requirements listed for each project are based on 43"/44" wide fabric with a "usable" width of 40" after shrinkage and trimming selvages. Actual usable width will probably vary slightly from fabric to fabric. Our recommended yardage lengths should be adequate for occasional re-squaring of fabric when many cuts are required.

PREPARING FABRICS
We recommend that all fabrics be washed, dried, and pressed before cutting. Bright and dark colors, which may run, should always be washed before cutting.

ROTARY CUTTING
Most of the pieces for the projects in this book can be rotary cut.
- Fold fabric lengthwise with wrong sides together and matching selvages.
- Remove selvage edges using rotary cutter and ruler.
- Place fabric on work surface with fold closest to you.

- Square left edge of fabric using rotary cutter and rulers (**Figs. 1–2**).

Fig. 1

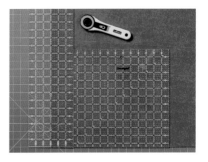

Fig. 2

- To cut each piece required for a project, place ruler over cut edge of fabric, aligning desired marking on ruler with cut edge; make cut (**Fig. 3**).

Fig. 3

Fig. 5

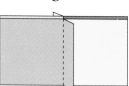

Sewing Sharp Points

To ensure sharp points when joining triangular or diagonal pieces, stitch across the center of the "X" (shown in pink) formed on wrong side by previous seams (**Fig. 6**).

Fig. 6

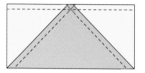

PRESSING

- Use steam iron set on setting appropriate for fabric being used. *Note:* For Minkee™ fabrics, which are polyester, a hot iron will easily damage the plush textures. Finger press or use a low temperature iron and press on the wrong side of the fabric.
- Press after sewing each seam.
- If using nylon webbing, do not touch iron to webbing.

PRESSING WHEN PIECING

- Seam allowances are almost always pressed to one side, usually toward darker fabric. However, to reduce bulk it may occasionally be necessary to press seam allowances toward the lighter fabric or even to press them open.
- To prevent dark fabric seam allowance from showing through light fabric, trim darker seam allowance slightly narrower than lighter seam allowance.

- When cutting several pieces from a single piece of fabric, it is important to make sure that cuts remain at a perfect right angle to the fold; square fabric as needed.

SEWING

Precise cutting, followed by accurate sewing, will ensure that all pieces of your project will fit together well.

- Set sewing machine stitch length for approximately 11 stitches per inch.
- Use matching or neutral-colored general-purpose sewing thread (not quilting thread) in needle and in bobbin.
- An accurate seam allowance is *essential*.
- When sewing, place pieces right sides together and match raw edges unless otherwise noted; pin if necessary.

PIECING

Sewing small fabric shapes, such as squares, triangles, or rectangles, together to form larger shapes is called piecing. For example, the stars in the You're Invited set, page 47, as well as the entire quilt top in that set, are all pieced.

Trimming Points

Trim away points of seam allowances that extend beyond edges of sewn pieces (**Fig. 4**).

Fig. 4

Sewing Across Seam Intersections

When sewing across intersection of two seams, place pieces right sides together and match seams exactly, making sure seam allowances are pressed in opposite directions (**Fig. 5**).

MACHINE APPLIQUÉ

The appliquéd designs on My Soft Blocks, page 43, are machine appliquéd using a zigzag stitch.

1. Pin stabilizer, such as paper or any of the commercially available products, on wrong side of background fabric before stitching appliqués in place.

2. Thread sewing machine with general-purpose thread or use clear mono-filament thread; use general-purpose thread that matches the background fabric in bobbin.

3. Set sewing machine for a medium (approximately $1/8$") zigzag stitch and a medium stitch length. Slightly loosening the top tension may yield a smoother stitch.

4. Begin by stitching two or three stitches in place (drop feed dogs or set stitch length at 0) to anchor thread. Most of the zigzag stitch should be on the appliqué with the right edge of the stitch falling at the outside edge of the appliqué. Stitch over all exposed raw edges of appliqué pieces.

5. (*Note:* Dots on **Figs. 7 – 12** indicate where to leave needle in fabric when pivoting.) For outside corners, stitch just past corner, stopping with needle in background fabric (**Fig. 7**). Raise presser foot. Pivot project, lower presser foot, and stitch adjacent side (**Fig. 8**).

Fig. 7

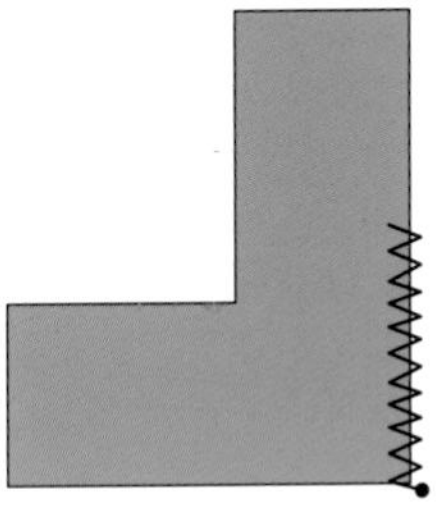

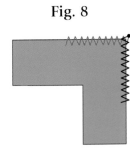

Fig. 8

6. For inside corners, stitch just past corner, stopping with needle in appliqué fabric (**Fig. 9**). Raise presser foot. Pivot project, lower presser foot, and stitch adjacent side (**Fig. 10**).

Fig. 9   **Fig. 10**

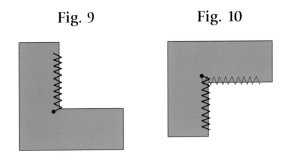

7. When stitching outside curves, stop with needle in background fabric. Raise presser foot and pivot project as needed. Lower presser foot and continue stitching, pivoting as often as necessary to follow curve (**Fig. 11**).

Fig. 11

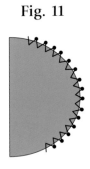

8. When stitching inside curves, stop with needle in appliqué fabric. Raise presser foot and pivot project as needed. Lower presser foot and continue stitching, pivoting as often as necessary to follow curve (**Fig. 12**).

Fig. 12

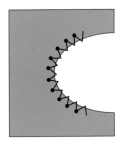

9. Do not backstitch at end of stitching. Pull threads to wrong side of background fabric; knot thread and trim ends.
10. Carefully tear away stabilizer.

QUILTING

Quilting holds the three layers (top, batting, and backing) of a quilt or quilted fabric piece (such as a tote front or flap) together. Please read entire **Quilting** *section, pages 75–76, before beginning your project.*

MARKING QUILTING LINES

Quilting lines may be marked using fabric marking pencils, chalk markers, or water- or air-soluble pens.

Simple quilting designs may be marked with chalk or chalk pencil after basting. A small area may be marked, then quilted, before moving to next area to be marked. Intricate designs should be marked before basting using a more durable marker.

Caution: Pressing may permanently set some marks. **Test** different markers **on scrap fabric** to find one that marks clearly and can be thoroughly removed.

PREPARING THE QUILT BACKING

To allow for slight shifting of quilt top during quilting, the quilt backing should be approximately 4" larger on all sides.
1. Measure length and width of quilt top; add 8" to each measurement.
2. Cut backing fabric into two lengths slightly longer than determined *length* measurement. Trim selvages. Place lengths with right sides facing and sew long edges together, forming tube (**Fig. 13**). Match seams and press along one fold (**Fig. 14**). Cut along pressed fold to form single piece (**Fig. 15**).

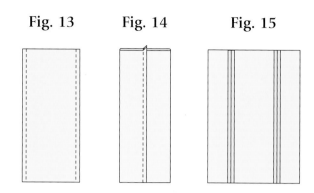

Fig. 13   Fig. 14   Fig. 15

3. Trim backing to size determined in Step 1; press seam allowances open.

ASSEMBLING THE QUILT LAYERS

Before quilting, you will need to assemble the layers (top, batting, and backing) of your quilt.
1. Examine wrong side of quilt top closely; trim any seam allowances and clip any threads that may show through front of the quilt. Press quilt top, being careful not to "set" any marked quilting lines.
2. Place backing *wrong* side up on flat surface. Use masking tape to tape edges of backing to surface.
3. Place batting on top of backing fabric. Smooth batting gently, being careful not to stretch or tear. Center quilt top *right* side up on batting.
4. Use 1" rustproof safety pins to "pin-baste" all layers together, spacing pins approximately 4" apart. Begin at center and work toward outer edges to secure all layers. If possible, place pins away from areas that will be quilted, although pins may be removed as needed when quilting.

MACHINE QUILTING METHODS

Use general-purpose thread in bobbin. Do not use quilting thread. Thread the needle of machine with general-purpose thread or transparent monofilament thread to make quilting blend with quilt top fabrics. Use decorative thread, such as a metallic or contrasting-color general-purpose thread, to make quilting lines stand out more.

Straight-Line Quilting

The term "straight-line" is somewhat deceptive, since curves (especially gentle ones) as well as straight lines can be stitched with this technique.

1. Set stitch length for six to ten stitches per inch and attach walking foot to sewing machine.
2. Determine which section of quilt sandwich will have longest continuous quilting line, oftentimes area from center top to center bottom. Roll up and secure each edge of quilt sandwich if needed to help reduce the bulk, keeping fabrics smooth.
3. Begin stitching on longest quilting line, using very short stitches for the first $1/4$" to "lock" quilting. Stitch across project, using one hand on each side of walking foot to slightly spread fabric and to guide fabric through machine. Lock stitches at end of quilting line.
4. Continue machine quilting, stitching longer quilting lines first to stabilize quilt sandwich before moving on to other areas.

Free-Motion Quilting

Free-motion quilting may be free form or may follow a marked pattern.

1. Attach darning foot to sewing machine and lower or cover feed dogs.
2. Position quilt under darning foot; lower foot. Holding top thread, take a stitch and pull bobbin thread to top of quilt. To "lock" beginning of quilting line, hold top and bobbin threads while making three to five stitches in place.

3. Use one hand on each side of darning foot to slightly spread fabric and to move fabric through the machine. Even stitch length is achieved by using smooth, flowing hand motion and steady machine speed. Slow machine speed and fast hand movement will create long stitches. Fast machine speed and slow hand movement will create short stitches. Move quilt sandwich sideways, back and forth, in a circular motion, or in a random motion to create desired designs; do not rotate quilt sandwich. Lock stitches at end of each quilting line.

MAKING A CONTINUOUS BIAS STRIP

Bias strips for binding can simply be cut and pieced to desired length. However, when a long length of bias strip is needed, the "continuous" method is quick and accurate.

1. Use the square for binding called for in project. Cut this square in half diagonally to make two triangles.
2. With right sides together and using a $1/4$" seam allowance, sew triangles together (**Fig. 16**); press seam allowances open.

Fig. 16

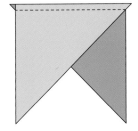

3. On wrong side of fabric, draw lines the width of bias strip as specified in project instructions (**Fig. 17**).

Fig. 17

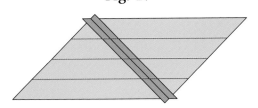

4. With right sides inside, bring short edges together to form tube; match raw edges so that first drawn line of top section meets second drawn line of bottom section (**Fig. 18**).

Fig. 18

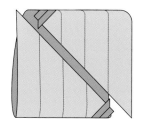

5. Carefully pin edges together by inserting pins through drawn lines at points where drawn lines intersect, making sure pins go through intersections on both sides. Using a $^1/_4$" seam allowance, sew edges together; press seam allowances open.
6. To cut continuous strip, begin cutting along first drawn line (**Fig. 19**). Continue cutting along drawn line around tube.

Fig. 19

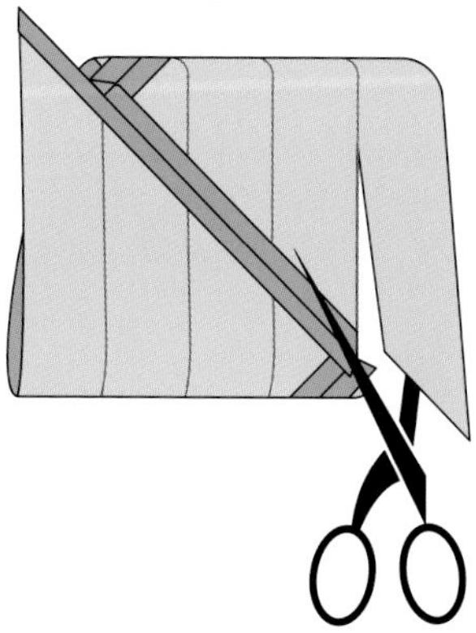

7. Trim ends of bias strip square.

BINDING
Binding is used to cover raw edges and give a finished look to your project.

ATTACHING BINDING
For any of the following methods of attaching binding, unless indicated otherwise, you will first sew the raw edges of the binding to the "wrong" or lining side of the project and bring the folded edge to the "right" or outer side and topstitch in place (**Fig. 20**).

Fig. 20

When binding seam allowances on the inside of a project, you may sew the raw edges of the seam binding to either side of the seam allowances first. Fold seam binding over raw edges and topstitch in place.

ATTACHING CONTINUOUS BINDING
Continuous binding is used where there is no visible beginning or end, such as on the top of a tote or around the edges of Quick Change Diaper Clutch, page 27.
1. Press 1 end of binding diagonally (**Fig. 21**).

Fig. 21

2. Matching raw edges and beginning with pressed end of binding on wrong/lining side of project, pin binding around raw edge of project.

3. Using a $^1/_4$" seam allowance, sew binding to project, until binding overlaps beginning end by about 2". Trim excess binding.

4. Fold binding to right side, covering stitching line and pin in place.

5. Topstitch binding in place close to folded edge.

ATTACHING OPEN END BINDING

Open end binding is used when the raw ends of a bound edge will be caught in a seam or covered by another strip of binding in a later step.

1. Matching raw edges, pin a length of binding along one edge of project. Using a $^1/_4$" seam allowance, sew binding to project (**Fig. 22**).

Fig. 22

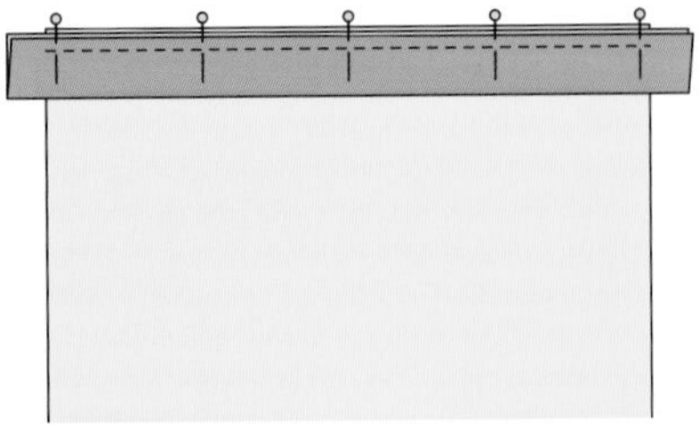

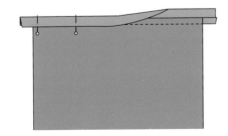

2. Fold binding over seam allowance, covering stitching line, and pin pressed edge in place (**Fig. 23**).

Fig. 23

3. Topstitch binding in place close to pressed edge.

4. Trim raw ends of binding even with edges of project.

ATTACHING CLOSED END BINDING

Closed end binding is used when the seam to be bound will not be caught or covered by another seam in a later step.

1. Matching raw edges and leaving approximately $^1/_2$" of binding extending at end(s), pin a length of binding along edge of project (**Fig. 24**).

Fig. 24

2. Using a $^1/_4$" seam allowance, sew binding to project (**Fig. 25**).

Fig. 25

3. Fold under raw end(s) of binding (**Fig. 26**); pin in place. Fold binding over seam allowance, covering stitching line, and pin folded edge in place (**Fig. 27**).

Fig. 26

Fig. 27

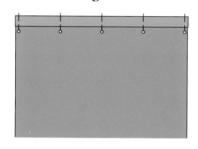

4. Topstitch binding in place close to pressed edge.

ATTACHING BINDING WITH MITERED CORNERS

Binding with mitered corners is used when a quilt or other project has 90° angled corners. These instructions are written for binding a quilt.

1. Press 1 end of binding diagonally (**Fig. 28**).

Fig. 28

2. Beginning with pressed end near center on bottom edge of quilt, lay binding around quilt to make sure that seams in binding will not end up at a corner. Adjust placement if necessary. Matching raw edges of binding to raw edge of quilt top, pin binding to right side of quilt along 1 edge.

3. When you reach first corner of quilt top, mark 1/4" from edge (**Fig. 29**).

Fig. 29

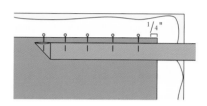

4. Using a 1/4" seam allowance, sew binding to quilt, backstitching at beginning of stitching and at mark (**Fig. 30**). Lift needle out of fabric and clip thread.

Fig. 30

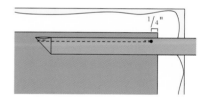

5. Fold binding as shown in **Figs. 31–32** and pin binding to adjacent side, matching raw edges. When you've reached the next corner of quilt top, mark 1/4" from edge.

Fig. 31   **Fig. 32**

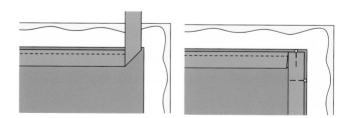

6. Backstitching at edge of quilt top, sew pinned binding to quilt (**Fig. 33**); backstitch at the next mark. Lift needle out of fabric and clip thread.

Fig. 33

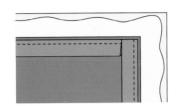

7. Continue sewing binding to quilt until binding overlaps beginning end by about 2". Trim excess binding.
8. Trim batting and backing a scant ¹/₄" larger than quilt top so that batting and backing will fill the binding when it is folded over to quilt backing.
9. On one edge of quilt, fold binding over to quilt backing and pin pressed edge in place, covering stitching line (**Fig. 34**). On adjacent side, fold binding over, forming a mitered corner (**Fig. 35**). Fold and pin remainder of binding in place.

Fig. 34   **Fig. 35**

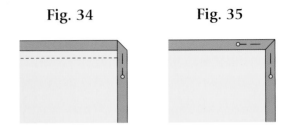

10. Blindstitch (**Fig. 36**) binding to backing, taking care not to stitch through to front of quilt. For Blindstitch, come up at 1, go down at 2, and come up at 3. Length of stitches may be varied as desired.

Fig. 36

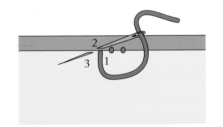

Metric Conversion Chart	
Inches x 2.54 = centimeters (cm)	Yards x .9144 = meters (m)
Inches x 25.4 = millimeters (mm)	Yards x 91.44 = centimeters (cm)
Inches x .0254 = meters (m)	Centimeters x .3937 = inches (")
	Meters x 1.0936 = yards (yd)

Standard Equivalents					
¹/₈"	3.2 mm	0.32 cm	¹/₈ yard	11.43 cm	0.11 m
¹/₄"	6.35 mm	0.635 cm	¹/₄ yard	22.86 cm	0.23 m
³/₈"	9.5 mm	0.95 cm	³/₈ yard	34.29 cm	0.34 m
¹/₂"	12.7 mm	1.27 cm	¹/₂ yard	45.72 cm	0.46 m
⁵/₈"	15.9 mm	1.59 cm	⁵/₈ yard	57.15 cm	0.57 m
³/₄"	19.1 mm	1.91 cm	³/₄ yard	68.58 cm	0.69 m
⁷/₈"	22.2 mm	2.22 cm	⁷/₈ yard	80 cm	0.8 m
1"	25.4 mm	2.54 cm	1 yard	91.44 cm	0.91 m